To Explain It All

To Explain It All

Everything You Wanted to Know about the Popularity of World History Today

Volume 2

Chris Edwards

ROWMAN & LITTLEFIELD
Lanham • Boulder • New York • London

Published by Rowman & Littlefield
An imprint of The Rowman & Littlefield Publishing Group, Inc.
4501 Forbes Boulevard, Suite 200, Lanham, Maryland 20706
https://rowman.com

6 Tinworth Street, London SE11 5AL, United Kingdom

Copyright © 2020 by Chris Edwards

All rights reserved. No part of this book may be reproduced in any form or by any electronic or mechanical means, including information storage and retrieval systems, without written permission from the publisher, except by a reviewer who may quote passages in a review.

British Library Cataloguing in Publication Information Available

Library of Congress Cataloging-in-Publication Data

Includes bibliographic references.
ISBN 978-1-4758-5590-6 (cloth)
ISBN 978-1-4758-5591-3 (pbk.)
ISBN 978-1-4758-5592-0 (electronic

Dedication

For Blake and Ben, who have the whole world in front of them.

Contents

Acknowledgments	ix
Introduction	1
1 World History through Islam	5
2 The Silk Roads: A New History of the World	33
3 A People's History of the World	55
4 Francis Fukuyama's Political Theory of World History	83
5 World History in Academia and the Development of Big History	125
Conclusion: World History for Education and Analogical Thinking	143
References	147
About the Author	149

Acknowledgments

Thanks to Charlie Guthrie for the conversations that helped to make these two volumes possible. As always, my editors Tom Koerner and Carlie Wall deserve a big thank-you for their professionalism and advice.

Introduction

Any introduction to a second volume should include a few words about the book that preceded it. Volume 1 of this endeavor included a narration of the field of world history (to be a work of history, the Americas must be included and this excludes any classical work) from its origin in 1920 with the publication of *The Outline of History* by H. G. Wells. That book analyzed different approaches to what may be loosely called the "traditional" history of the world. The "traditional" history of the world treats Western civilization as a protagonist in the development of the modern era. Much was written about world history in volume 1, but the most important words came in the conclusion, where I admitted a feeling of inadequacy regarding the analysis of this varied and voluminous topic. The conceit that shaped that first volume was that *an* analysis of the field of world history is better than *no* analysis of the field of world history. That sentiment links volume 1 with this one.

A few points from volume 1's purpose should be repeated here: 1) world history does not fit well with traditional historical methods; 2) world history is the leading candidate for a unified field of knowledge; 3) polymaths who have operated in cross-curricular disciplines have begun to tout a "big history" as the leading candidate to unify knowledge and to adapt new forms of cross-curricular and analogical thought; 4) because of this, an analysis of the field and its various approaches helps to fill an important gap in the scholarship. Hence these books.

A work comes in two or more volumes when the topic is either too big or too varied to be handled in a single volume. World history is certainly a big topic, but the subject's variability is what makes a two-volume structure necessary; to transition from analysis of "traditional" Western-oriented histories of the world to the nontraditional histories would likely be to create a narrative that would jar the reader halfway through if the topic was handled in a single book. These are the justifications for the project and its two-volume structure.

Volume 2 will follow a pattern of analysis that is similar to that of the first book. The first four chapters analyze "alternative" histories of the world; these are works that attempt to tell the story of world history with a non-Western narrative arc. These histories fit within the traditional boundaries of "history" in the sense that they do not include a study of the scientific endeavors of astrophysics, geology, archaeology, biology, and demography that are the mark of so-called Big History.

One point should be made here regarding these four chapters. Readers might occasionally wonder if I have not fallen into the age-old book reviewer's fallacy of arguing that authors should have written a different book than what they did. The scope of this two-volume project is larger than a series of book reviews; my purpose is to clarify a proper logical approach to world historical studies, and this sometimes needs to be done by critiquing false approaches and by culling back unserious research and writing.

There a few books with "world history" in the title that are not included for analysis in this volume, and their exclusion deserves an explanation. Lincoln Paine's *The Sea and Civilization: A Maritime History of the World* (2013) is finely constructed and a pleasure to read; it was just christened with the wrong subtitle. Paine's book should be subtitled "Maritime History *in* the World," as Paine's objective is to expand upon traditional land-based histories by showing the importance of sea- and ocean-based trade and power networks.

Mark Booth's *The Secret History of the World* (2007) has the same problem, as does Neil Faulkner's *A Radical History of the World* (2013). Booth only writes about secret societies and their roles in different places and time periods, and Faulkner's book would be better titled "Radicalism in World History." I would recommend all three of these books to potential readers and believe that all of them make contributions to world historical studies. None of these books, however, attempts to "explain it all" regarding world history, only certain parts of it.

Chapter 5 details the development of a separate evolutionary branch of world history, one that spreads into fields more often seen as scientific. This section will be about William McNeill and the place of world history in the academy and in education in general. The evolution away from traditional historical methods eventually led to a new term of classification, that of Big History.

The promise of Big History is in the unification of knowledge under a monolithic heading for the purpose of telling a single overarching historical narrative. Physicists tried something similar a century ago only to see the endeavor collapse under the weight of probability theory; Big History's internal contradictions, along with the cut-and-paste approach that its scholars (educated as historians) take with the actual science, have prevented and will continue to prevent the concept from connecting the disciplines.

The conclusion of this book will propose that the purpose of world history should not be to create a single overarching narrative for the creation of everything. World history also cannot sustain the pressure that comes from trying to unite all the fields into a single discipline. Instead world history should be recognized for its potential in teaching cross-curricular thinking for the purpose of developing novel analogies.

A history of world history in education will be traced here, and scholarly works involving world historical studies will be integrated into this section as a way of describing world history's practical relevance. My own work in creating world historical curricula will be explained in this section but not analyzed. Recommendations regarding the understanding of world history's purpose and presentation will be made in this final section as well.

In volume 1, I made a point of quoting the Greek writer Polybius (264–146 BCE), who explained the advantages of the broader historical approach (it can't be called a "world" historical approach during his time period because Polybius did not know that another half of the world existed). Polybius stated that the disadvantage of the traditional historical method of developing a research question and then exhausting the topic in search of evidence was that that method "omits events in parallel." In other words, by just studying one time period and one area, one misses out on the connections that could be made by a broader analysis.

Volume 2 starts with the words of another historian, the "Venerable" Bede (673–735), the historian and ecclesiastic of England who wrote, "study, teaching, and writing have always been my delight." To study about, to teach about, and to write about world history *is* a delight, and my hope is that readers will sense that joy as they read this second volume regarding a topic that has provided me with the same kind of emotion expressed by Bede.

NON-WESTERN HISTORIES OF THE WORLD

In keeping with the title of this two-volume work, a true world history seeks "to explain it all" and therefore the author must attempt, in his or her narrative, to connect and explain all the regions of the world from some point in prehistory to roughly the present. For the first four chapters, four works with alternative narrations not aligned with the "ascent of the West" theme will be analyzed. The works are (1) *Destiny Disrupted: A History of the World through Islamic Eyes* (2009) by Tamim Ansary, (2) *The Silk Roads: A New History of the World* (2015) by Peter Frankopan, (3) *A People's History of the World: From the Stone Age to the New Millennium* (1999) by Chris Harman, and (4) *The Origins of Political Order: From Prehuman Times to the French Revolution* (2011) and *Political Order and Political Decay: From the Industrial Revolution to the Globalization of Democracy* (2014), both by Francis Fukuyama.

There's no reason for the order of the analyses here except that Francis Fukuyama's two-volume work will come last because his approach connects to the concluding themes of this volume and therefore provides the most natural connection to the next section of this book.

ONE
World History through Islam

Is a history of the world from the perspective of a religious group possible? No Christian philosopher ever created a world history out of purely biblical sources. Sir Walter Raleigh (1552–1618) cobbled together a timeline of sorts from ancient sources, but he did this while imprisoned in the Tower of London, and the writing of the book probably served to distract his mind from the premonition of a falling axe more than it served scholarship. Raleigh's "world history" remains unfinished. Tamim Ansary's approach is different from Raleigh's in that Ansary is not treating the Old Testament as actual history but rather is trying to develop a world history without a Eurocentric/Western orientation.

In the first two introductory paragraphs of his book *Destiny Disrupted: A History of the World through Islamic Eyes*, the writer (he is careful, as so many writers of history are, to note that he is not a scholar) Tamim Ansary states that he hails from Afghanistan where he developed an interest in reading books of history in English while still a young man. At some point, he read a history of the world that was written for a young audience and later, as an adult, read the book again and "realized how shockingly Eurocentric it was, how riddled with casual racism" (2010, xxiii).

Ansary understands the "traditional" narrative of world history in this way:

1. Birth of Civilization (Egypt and Mesopotamia)
2. Classical Age (Greece and Rome)
3. The Dark Ages (rise of Christianity)
4. The Rebirth: Renaissance and Reformation
5. The Enlightenment (exploration and science)
6. The Revolutions (democratic, industrial, technological)
7. Rise of Nation-States: The Struggle for Empire

8. World Wars I and II
9. The Cold War
10. The Triumph of Democratic Capitalism. (2010, xix)

Ansary seems to be equating "world history" with an outline for a Western civilization course. From the beginning of the field of world history, the practitioners sought to balance the narrative of Western civilization by including regions outside of the West and by studying the effects that the West eventually imposed on those areas. Ansary seems, right away, to misunderstand what world history as a discrete subject of study really is.

The "ascent of the West" conceit does contain these ten points, but from a world historical vantage, those points can only be explained through the West's more global interactions. Item number 4 on Ansary's list, "The Rebirth: Renaissance and Reformation," could not have occurred without the East-West connection established through Crusader routes to the Islamic world, scholarly interchange in Al-Andalus (the medieval and Muslim-controlled Iberian Peninsula), and the thirteenth-century Mongol conquests.

Anasary's book must be, by virtue of its title and subject matter, based on the axiom that world histories written by people in the Western world must be naturally biased toward the "Triumph of Democratic Capitalism." Western intellectuals in the Noam Chomsky tradition sometimes engage in overt and over-the-top criticisms of, say, the United States and its foreign policies as a way of trying to prove that they, the intellectuals, are not trapped by some kind of bias toward Western civilization.

The problem with stating that the "Triumph of Democratic Capitalism" contains some kind of bias comes from any study of modern global history at any time. In 1919, women and their male allies across the United States marched in the streets and wrote to the papers in advocacy for a constitutional guarantee that women could vote. One hundred years later, exactly no one is out in the streets advocating that this amendment be repealed.

In 1956, the Hungarians, chafing under Soviet domination, advocated in the streets for the granting of greater levels of political freedom. The Russians drove tanks over them as a way of demonstrating that military terror held the USSR together. No American tanks ever rolled over anyone of the North Atlantic Treaty Organization; it was a voluntary organization.

In 1989, thousands of dissidents against single-party Communist rule organized and protested their regime in Tiananmen Square, and Communist thugs responded with the old tank-treads-on-your-face tactic they normally used. At no time, anywhere, have American or British demonstrators ever advocated that democratic government be disbanded in favor of single-party Communist rule. If anyone ever did get this notion, they could demonstrate freely without fear of government attack.

If these arguments seem simplistic, then that's because the lesson is simple. People tend to like personal freedom and democratic participation. Democratic capitalism as a triumph is not a Western narrative to world history but a demonstrable historical fact. Democratic capitalism just happened to occur in the West, but it's a universal system.

Still, the reader gets Ansary's point. World history tends to trend toward a Western conception of politics. What, then, would an outline of world history from the perspective of Muslims look like? He writes:

> If the stunted present experienced by Islamic society is taken as the here-and-now to be explained by the narrative of world history, then the story might break down to something like the following stages:
>
> 1. Ancient times: Mesopotamia and Persia
> 2. Birth of Islam
> 3. The Khalifate: Quest for Universal Unity
> 4. Fragmentation: Age of the Sultanates
> 5. Catastrophe: Crusaders and Mongols
> 6. Rebirth: The Three Empires Era
> 7. Permeation of East by West
> 8. The Reform Movements
> 9. Triumph of Secular Modernists
> 10. The Islamist Reaction. (2010, xx)

Points 7 through 10 explain, ultimately, why Ansary sets himself up for failure in his endeavor. "Permeation of the East by the West" indicates that Western civilization developed an internal force that allowed them to burst into the empires of the East and dictate the political and cultural terms. By stating "The Reform Movements" as a reaction, Ansary shows that the Islamic societies had to form again in a different mold that was created by forces in the West. "Triumph of Secular Modernists" can be seen, again, as reaction to a cultural and legal norm, that of secularism, that formed historically in the West.

Finally, the phrase "The Islamist Reaction" refers again to the essentially passive nature of Islamic society when faced with the dynamism of the West. The nature of a "reaction" is, ultimately, passive at first and active only in the sense that a change has been forced by a more assertive actor.

Inevitably, popular books such as this include some kind caveat about the author's qualifications:

> *Destiny Disrupted* is neither a textbook nor a scholarly thesis. It's not like what I'd tell you if we met in a coffeehouse and you said, "What's all this about a parallel world history?" The argument I make can be found in numerous books now on the shelves of university libraries.

> Read it there if you don't mind the academic language and footnotes. Read it here if you want the story arc. Although I am not a scholar, I have drawn on the work of scholars who sift the raw material of history to draw conclusion and of academics who sifted the work of scholarly researchers to draw meta-conclusions. (2010, xxi)

What are the "numerous books now on the shelves of university libraries"? Is Ansary speaking of scholarly works about the Islamic world or about works of world history? The bibliography of *Destiny Disrupted* contains no actual works about world history, not even the popular one-volume work by J. M. Roberts that would seem to be a natural place to start for someone looking to obtain a "traditional" world history for the purpose of countering it with a world history not aligned to the Western civilization.

Ansary's claim to not be a scholar should not trouble him or the reader; world history does not produce scholars in the same manner than an ordinary historical field would. The claim itself serves only to shield the author from criticisms regarding the book's lack of original historical thinking. Early on, Ansary critiques the phrase "Middle East" because "Middle East assumes that one is standing in Western Europe. . . . Therefore, I prefer to call this whole area from the Indus to Istanbul the Middle World, because it lies between the Mediterranean world and the Chinese world" (2010, 3).

It's never clear what the purpose of such renaming gestures such as this is. The consensus date modifier change from BC (Before Christ) to BCE (Before Common Era) and AD (Anno Domini) to CE (Common Era) did nothing to aid anyone's understanding of historical chronology and actually draws attention away from the important fact that the Christian calendar contains within it a specific history of its own that was connected to Christendom. All world maps and globes likewise feature a bias toward to the northern hemisphere. We know that the phrase "Middle East" came from a European perspective already.

What follows is a history of the Mesopotamian region seemingly cut from the work of Alfred Crosby and Jared Diamond (neither is listed in the bibliography). China and the Americas, because mountains and deserts in the first case and the Atlantic and Pacific Oceans in the second, remained isolated from the main interplay of communication in the "Middle World." This is important because "perhaps the most dynamic petri dish of early human culture was that fertile wedge of land between the Tigris and Euphrates known as Mesopotamia—which means, in fact, 'between the rivers'" (2010, 4).

Readers looking for an Islamic viewpoint regarding world history might grow impatient, even irritated, with the pre-Islamic history of the region, and Ansary's authorial instinct was to keep this first chapter short. The concept of early regions of the world being "petri dishes" for historical and cultural experimentation is fairly well known.

This first chapter on the "Middle World" mostly establishes the place of Islam's future ethnic groups in their proper geographic places. For example, "By the time the Persians took charge, around 550 BCE, a lot of consolidation had already been done: in each region, earlier conquerors had drawn various local tribes and towns into single systems ruled by one monarch from a central capital, whether Elam, Ur, Nineveh, or Babylon" (2010, 7). The Persians are mentioned here as a precursor to the Islamic Empires that are understood to be coming.

The virtues of the Persian Empire, according to Ansary, included:

> a multicultural, many-people-under-one-big-tent strategy. They controlled their enormous realm by letting all the different constituent peoples live their own lives according to their own folkways and mores, under the rule of their own leaders, provided they paid their taxes and submitted to a few of the emperor's mandates and demands. The Muslims later picked up on this idea, and it persisted through Ottoman times. (2010, 8)

Focus on the word "multicultural." Broken into two dry etymological pieces, the word simply means "more than two cultures," but the word contains a further context that includes the idea that disparate and sometimes oppositional cultures should at least tolerate each other and sometimes even celebrate each other. To use the term in conjunction with empires of any kind is to misunderstand what an empire is.

For a political entity to be an empire, a core group, defined by religion, ethnicity, nationality, or some other random form of categorization, must impose an asymmetric political relationship on groups not included in the core. Asymmetric relations are established with noncore groups through an imbalance in either military capability or economic and trading influences.

The "multiculturalism" of an empire can only come when noncore peoples are forced, through circumstance, to provide conscript labor or excess taxation to the core group. Multiculturalism in its modern sense (and it only has a modern sense) simply cannot apply to any empire, and its usage makes little sense in a conversation about either Persia or later Islam.

Ansary does well to exit the first chapter as quickly as possible because his understanding of world historical events seems unstable; he writes as if in a hurry to establish a few sophomoric points about Eurocentrism and then the types of cultures that would eventually be enveloped by Islam. Consider this passage:

> Almost any well-educated Westerner knows of Socrates, Plato, and Aristotle, not to mention Sophocles, Virgil, Tacitus, Pericles, Alexander of Macedon, Julius Caesar, Augustus, and many others; but apart from

academics who specialize in Byzantine history, few can name three Byzantine philosophers, or two Byzantine poets, or one Byzantine emperor after Justinian. The Byzantine Empire lasted almost a thousand years, by [sic] few can name five events that took place in the empire during that time.

Compared to ancient Rome, the Byzantine Empire didn't wield much clout, but in its own region it was a superpower, largely because it had no competition and because its walled capital of Constantinople was probably the most impregnable city the world [has] ever known. (2010, 14)

Such sentiments reveal that Ansary likely never intended to develop a true world history, and such a thing as a *History of the World through Islamic Eyes* makes as little sense as a history of the world through Mormon eyes; one would have to dismiss the history that existed before the religion as insignificant or as being a precursor to the arrival of the very peoples through which the vantage point is shown. This seems to be exactly the tactic that Ansary intends to employ, and it is both irresponsible historically and indefensible as a literary device.

The dismissal of the Byzantine Empire as a historical force is justified, somehow, because the hypothetical "well-educated Westerner" that Ansary builds up as a caricature would not know much about the topic. This is just lazy thinking and demonstrates a lack of knowledge about the interplay of the Byzantines, the Persians, and later Muslims in the reconstruction of Central Asia's political configurations after the arrival of Islam.

First, the notion that Western-educated elites would dismiss the Byzantine Empire as important might have held up until forty or fifty years ago. The 1979 reprint (via Penguin Classics) of *Fourteen Byzantine Rulers* by the Byzantine scholar and advisor Michael Psellus (1018–1096) contains these words:

The attitude to Byzantia nowadays has changed radically, thanks to the fine work of many scholars (Baines, Hussey, Talbot Rice, Gervase Mathew, Beckwith, Moss, and the historians Vailiev and Ostogorsky, to name only a few whose books have been published in English). The vigour and genius of Byzantine artists, who were in fact far from stereotyped or conventional, are now acclaimed. (2012, 10)

Between 1989 and 1995, John Julius Norwich published three volumes on the history of the empire that provided as much of a popular (that is to say "readable") narrative of the empire as the topic probably needs. No one who is serious about world history dismisses the Byzantine Empire, and historians of Islam should consider the empire itself to be a crucial factor in the development of early Dar-al-Islam.

Heraclius ruled the Byzantine Empire from 610 to 641; this was at the time when Mohammed supposedly existed, received his revelations from the angel Gabirl, spoke the Qu'ran, governed Medina, and conquered Mecca. During the first years of his tenure as emperor, Heraclius fought almost continually against the Persian (Sassanian) Empire of Chosroes II, and that war only ended in 627 with a Byzantine victory that left both empires in a state of financial and military exhaustion.

The historical parallel to the Byzantine-Persian war of the seventh century would be the Peloponnesian War (431–404 BCE) in the sense that the major Aegean powers of Sparta and Athens wore each other down over the course of nearly three decades of fighting. With the people in each city-state financially, military, and (perhaps) emotionally exhausted by war, a military niche suddenly opened. Phillip II (382–336 BCE) restructured the military of the northern city-state of Macedon using a variety of military innovations. By 338, Phillip led his new military in a conquest of Athens and Thebes. Phillip fell dead from a servant's blade just two years later and bequeathed his formative empire and formidable military to his twenty-year-old son Alexander (soon to be "the Great").

The conquests of Alexander the Great (356–323 BCE) need not be detailed here, but in just thirteen years, he beat the Spartans and repeatedly embarrassed the Persians on the battlefield. In the process, Alexander created the first empire that meant anything in terms of geographic scale. Several factors can be attributed to Alexander's military success, if it happened, but historical parallels indicate that the fallout of the Peloponnesian War rates as the most significant.

Islam's legitimacy came not from the words of Mohammed but from the rapid period of military conquest that followed Mohammed's death that provided justification by the sword for the veracity of those words. Mohammed's message (whatever its historical value) was/is arbitrary. Without the conquests that followed Mohammed's death in 632, he would have been forgotten in the same way that the prophetic words of Tenskwatawa (1775–1836) or Hong Xiuquian (1814–1864) have been.

To state all of this would require some actual world historical analysis, but this seems to be either outside of Ansary's area of expertise our outside of his purpose, so virtually nothing is said about the importance of Byzantium. This rather thorough rebuttal of a small section of the book might seem like an excessive response, but world history is a young field and therefore susceptible to being defined by inadequate scholarship.

Chapter 2 begins with the year 622, which happens to be the first year in Islam's lunar calendar. In popular works of history, a meta-analysis of the primary source material rarely occurs. This may be based on the assumption that a literate audience will understand that premodern source material can be expected to contain stories of fantasy. Still, Ansary marks no point of demarcation for his readers between modern historical analysis and premodern Arabic fantasy.

For example, this statement about pre-Islamic Arabia is based upon modern historical analyses: "most of the Arabs were pagan polytheists at this point and the Jews had remained resolutely monotheistic, the two groups were otherwise more or less indistinguishable in terms of culture and lifestyle: the Jews of this area spoke Arabic, and their tribal structure resembled that of the Arabs" (2010, 17).

No demarcation is made between the sober historical analysis that marks the discussion of pre-Islamic Arabia and Ansary's treatment of Mohammed's biography. The effect, for readers not familiar with the means of logical analytics, is to treat the modern historical sources and the Islamic historical sources as equally valid. Modern historians employ logic to treat historical events with certain levels of probability. If an ancient document includes a narrative of an event, then historians are trained to see if other forms of evidence corroborate that event.

David Hume (1711–1776), in his *An Enquiry Concerning Human Understanding* (1975), commented on the difference in probability between various statements. For example, if someone related a story in which she threw a ball into the air and the ball fell back to the ground, then the story would fit well with natural laws. This would increase the probability that the story contained truth. If she told a story in which she threw a ball into the air and it just kept going up into the sky, then she would either have a heck of a throwing arm or she would be lying to you. One would have to judge those probabilities against each other.

World historians often note that the Islamic world missed out on the Renaissance, Reformation, Scientific Revolution, Exploration, and the Enlightenment and that this explains why the Islamic historical trajectory stagnated at a time when the West developed into something new. The Muslims also missed out on the development of a proper historical method, that, by 1906 was also used on the foundational sources of the Christian faith. Christianity never produced a coherent world history, but it did produce a contained narrative that could be tested (and proved wanting) by historical methods.

Second, Islam's main text, the Qu'ran, contains nothing about the life of Mohammed and little in the way of a narrative can be derived from it. The Qu'ran makes no sense. It makes no sense in Arabic, English, French, or Russian. The text is impenetrable to any form of analysis because it represents a series of broken up monologues uttered at various times, in changing conditions, and written down and codified a few decades after the death of Mohammed.

The Qu'ran has never suffered from the analysis of an Islamic Albert Schweitzer because it makes no claims that can be verified or not verified by historical analysis. On one level of analysis, it is what it claims to be: the spoken words of a single illiterate Arabian man between the years of 610 and 632. On another level of analysis, it is unlikely to be what it claims to be, which is the unalterable word of God, because the Qu'ran contains no truths that would not have been understood by a single illiterate Arabian man who spoke between the years of 610 and 632.

No religious story can survive a logical test like this as the probability of a "miracle" occurring must always be balanced against the more likely scenario of a writer passing on fantastical tales. It has never been clear how much people of the past actually believed in the biblical stories; the Catholic Church never took all of the Bible literally, and the medieval masses to whom the priests said mass could not read and write anyway, but educated people could still express a vague belief in a creator deity at least up until the nineteenth century.

Darwin's description of the facts of biology rendered the Old Testament into an allegory (at best), but it was the work of a German philosopher, Albert Schweitzer, in 1906 that addressed the uncomfortable subject of the historicity regarding the life of Jesus. Schweitzer's book *Quest of the Historical Jesus* analyzed the gospels of the New Testament through the methods of a modern historian. Even if one accepted the existence and the words of Jesus as historical, wrote Schweitzer, Jesus preached the immediate arrival of a cataclysmic End Times. Those predictive words, certainly by 1906, could be proved wrong.

From Schweitzer to the present (the author/professor Bart Ehrman is Schweitzer's modern American equivalent), the methods of historical inquiry have wrought havoc on all of the Christian versions of biblical belief. Any church (including the Catholic) whose theologians profess to take sections of the Bible as allegory needs to explain why certain sections are taken as allegory and certain other sections are taken as literal.

Any church whose theologians take a literalist/fundamentalist stance would need to explain why the biblical stories never seem to be supported by modern scientific or historical evidence. Furthermore, why does the Bible not include any knowledge (not even of the Americas) that would not have been known by people who were living at the time that the books of the Bible were written?

All of this has to be said in order to say that the Islamic world never went through this process. While it is not uncommon for scholars in the modern West to point out that 1) the synoptic gospels were anonymously written, 2) the first of these gospels (likely Mark) was written about three decades after the death of Jesus, 3) the original versions of the gospels are lost, 4) the gospels were written in Greek while Jesus and his followers likely spoke Aramaic, and 5) at least twenty noncanonical gospels exist that never made it into the Bible. The Islamic sources are rarely ever scrutinized in such a way. There are reasons for this.

Mohammed's biography, the Sira, was not written until about one and a quarter centuries after his death. The author, Ibn Ishaq (704–773), derived his narrative from unknown source material. When Ishaq died, his book remained unknown and the first copy of his work disappeared. An abridged version of the original work, edited by a scholar named Ibn Hasham, later appeared and became a part of the Islamic canon. Islam's early history comes from this source and is supplemented by various texts from a supplementary collection of texts known as the Hadith.

The Hadith, as a whole, is a topic too complicated to be of use for the purposes of this chapter, but it provides a modicum of historical and cultural context for any scholar who attempts to impose some meaning onto the Qu'ran. The Hadith provides little overarching narrative as it is a collection of sayings, and there are different collections of these sayings that supposedly link back to the time of Mohammed.

Sunni and Shia scholars can get very involved in the texts of the Hadith and sometimes create elaborate arguments around the sayings, but the entirety of the Hadith is too contradictory and tangled to provide much in the way of an actual historical narrative. The purpose of the Hadith is to use the sayings to analyze the siras of the Qu'ran, not to give historians a clear timeline of events.

The three major historical texts (or series of texts) that make up the body of Islamic belief are the Qu'ran, the Sira, and the Hadith. Of these, only the Sira provides a clear narrative that might be defined as an attempt at history. One can understand why Islamic scholars would not want to submit the Sira to a logical scrutiny, but Ansary is claiming to write a book of history. This means that the historical veracity of such documents should be analyzed with logic and the historical method.

Instead he never mentions the Sira or Hadith and just blends the traditional, if spurious, historical narrative of Islam into his narrative without any explanation or justification:

> [Mohammed] developed a habit of retreating periodically to a cave in the mountains to meditate. There, one day, he had a momentous experience, the exact nature of which remains mysterious, since various accounts survive, possibly reflecting various descriptions by Mohammed himself. Tradition has settled on calling the experience a visitation from the angel Gabriel. In one account, Mohammed spoke of "a silken cloth on which was some writing" brought to him while he was asleep. In the main, however, it was apparently an oral and personal interaction, which started when Mohammed, meditating in the utter darkness of a cave, sensed an overwhelming and terrifying presence: someone else was in the cave with him. Suddenly he felt himself gripped from behind so hard he could not breathe. Then came a voice, not so much heard as felt through his being, commanding him to "recite!"
>
> Mohammed managed to gasp out that he could not recite.
>
> The command came again: "Recite!"
>
> Again Mohammed protested that he could not recite, did not know what to recite, but the angel-the voice- the impulse- blazed once more: "Recite!" Thereupon Mohammed felt words of terrible grandeur forming in his heard and the recitation began. (2010, 19)

Nothing about this section is historical, and it is revealing that even the footnote takes the reader to a secondary historical source. The history of Islam cannot be derived from the Sira or from Islamic texts because those texts fail every test of logic. Even if historians possessed compelling evidence that Mohammed existed and that he used to visit caves, the possibility that an angel grabbed him would have to be set against the possibility that the story was made up. If someone was grabbed by an emissary from an all-powerful deity, that person might be expected to have some knowledge beyond what an ordinary person would have known at the time.

The real history of Islam, like the real history of Judaism, Christianity, and Communism, is the story of how military conquest facilitated the construction of mythologies.

At some point in the seventh century, likely around the year 634, the warriors of the Arabian Peninsula rode out of the north and conquered west across North Africa and east into the Byzantine territories. This may or may not have had anything to do with a religion called Islam; certainly no Qu'ran existed at the time, and if Mohammed really was a historical figure, he had died. Not much else can be historically verified about the earliest years of Islam.

In the seventh century, the Arabic peoples (sometimes called Bedouins) lived a largely nomadic existence. Divided into clans, they fought constantly over watering holes and blood feuds. Situated east of the Red Sea, Arabia was also caddy cornered to the Mediterranean, and this meant that trade, culture, and religion could filter into cities like Mecca and Medina. A latent military potential must have been pulsing in the Arabian Peninsula for a long time as the camel- and horse-riding nomads developed military skills just from living and fighting in a harsh desert environment.

Certainly *something* united the Bedouin tribesman in the seventh century. However, what or who exactly united the Arabic nomads into a fighting force in the 630s is unclear. The unwritten words of a prophet probably played less of a unifying factor than did Byzantine and Persian weakness.

The most probable explanation for the sudden military expansion of Islam in the seventh century is that one of the constant and random wars that took place between tribal groups in the northern peninsula spilled out into North Africa. Bedouin warriors who captured cities and towns likely found unified purpose in a love of power and plunder (as all peoples seemed to) and expanded into regions where Byzantine and Persian power structures needed only a little pressure to collapse.

Seventh-century Arabic imperialism cannot be compared to the nineteenth-century European variety. The Arabs do not seem to have equated military supremacy with cultural supremacy. At this point, it is important to note that before the development of gunpowder weapons, the great civilizations of the world did not necessarily possess any kind of military advantage over the tribal "barbarians" who constantly threatened their borders.

In the modern era, it's impossible to imagine nomads on horses threatening a modern nation-state. This is because nation-states contain schools of science and engineering that lead to military power, and that process did not begin until the development of sophisticated gunpowder weapons in roughly the fourteenth century. In the seventh century, the sophisticates at the Byzantine and Persian courts would not necessarily have enjoyed any military advantage over the illiterate bumpkins riding into their cities. The Arabs, people of the desert, conquered a massive empire but found themselves gazing up at buildings and into cultures that must have made them feel lacking in something.

These are probably the conditions in which the Islamic mythology was then developed as an afterthought to the conquest. At this point, Mohammed was either invented or cobbled together from quasi-historical memory. If any coherent message can be derived from the Qu'ran at all, it is this: conquer, collect taxes, impose a nonsensical set of rituals that enforce the power structure, and then repeat. It's a message written by men for men, and the sensual afterlife that the Qu'ran infuses into the imaginations of male believers likely reflects the desires of the book's author or authors, whoever they were.

The fact that the Qu'ran was not written until about twenty years after Mohammed's death makes the conceit that it represents the exact words of anyone more than unlikely. The notion that historical and biographical accounts of Mohammed, written one hundred and twenty-five years after the events of Mohammed's life supposedly occurred, have any historical significance at all is in opposition to the entirety of scientific and historical methodology. Mohammed is a literary figure and the Qu'ran a piece of literature that is likely unrelated to any actual events that took place in the seventh-century Arabian Peninsula.

This point must be made in detail not only because it partially refutes Ansary's approach ("partially" refutes because his work has other problems) but also because this helps to set up one of the justifications for the "Big History" approach that will be analyzed later. "Big History" seeks to avoid the problem of the historical veracity of ancient sources by simply skipping them and generalizing about various "phases" of history.

Ansary treats the Islamic sources as historical sources, which is a flaw, but more importantly he sees the connection between the sources and the practices of Islam as something more than coincidental. Islamic literary tradition has it that Mohammed left Mecca and went north to Medina in 622, and this represents the first year in the Islamic calendar and an episode of extreme importance. "What makes moving from one town to another so momentous?" (2010, 23), asks Ansary.

The answer is that

this social project, which became fully evident in Medina . . . is a core element of Islam. Quite definitely, Islam is a religion, but right from the start . . . it was *also* a political entity. Yes, Islam prescribes a way to be good, and yes every devoted Muslim hopes to get into heaven by following that way, but instead of focusing on isolated individual salvation, Islam presents a plan for building a righteous community. Individuals earn their place in heaven by participating as members of that community and engaging in the Islamic social project, which is to build a world in which orphans won't feel abandoned and in which widows won't ever be homeless, hungry, or afraid. (2010, 24)

Almost nothing about this paragraph makes sense. Islam cannot be described as a "social project," at least not in a positive sense. With the exception of Indonesia, which was "converted" to a watery variation of the faith by traders in the thirteenth century, the entirety of the Islamic world was consolidated via conquest. This conquest was first completed by the Arabs, and then Persians, and Turks joined the Ummah as bureaucrats and warrior-slaves respectively. By the tenth century, as Arabic influence declined, the Persians and Turks increasingly became the Ummah's dominant ethnic group.

Right to the present, Arabic, Turkish, and Persian rivalry and conflict define Middle Eastern politics. Anyone who looks closely enough at Islam will eventually have to conclude that it doesn't actually exist as a coherent doctrine at all, much less a social project. Without a central theology, Islam is just a collection of vague texts. Islamic scholars issue *fatwahs* or religious rulings based on certain interpretations of the texts, and then Muslim believers either follow those or don't. Only when a particular interpretation of Islam is attached to the power of the state and the military can it be actually enforced on people as a "social project."

By noting that Islam does not focus on "individual salvation," it can be inferred that Ansary intends a comparison with Christianity. Only certain variations of Protestantism, only available after 1517, stressed this. The medieval church that existed concurrently with early Islam focused on the mass of believers and, in the West, functioned as a political entity in much the way Islam did, only more so.

Finally, while one can find much discussion about the treatment of orphans and widows in the Qu'ran, these passages are generally interpreted to only include people within the Ummah. Muslims are free to kill and enslave non-Muslims. It's not uncommon for any power structure reliant upon war to make provisions to care for widows and orphans as this helps to uphold popular approval for a military state. The same kind of provisions existed in the Mongol Empire and can be found in virtually every militaristic nation-state.

Some of Ansary's statements indicate that he does not understand Islam very well. One example is as follows: "Mohammed never claimed supernatural powers. He never claimed the ability to raise the dead, walk on water, or make the blind to see. He only claimed to speak for God, and he didn't claim that every word out of his mouth was God talking. Sometimes it was just Mohammed talking. How could people tell when it was God and when it was Mohammed?" (2010, 29).

How, exactly, is the ability to "speak for God" not a supernatural power? That would seem to be something more than natural. Furthermore, an Islamic tradition that's stitched together from the Qu'ran and Hadith has it that, in 621, Mohammed rode on a winged horse to heaven and met Moses. A close reading of the source material makes it difficult to understand how the story was derived from the Qu'ranic verses, but to restate an important point, the Qu'ran is incoherent and so one could derive just about *any* meaning from it.

Ansary's approach to the sources of Islam is irresponsible and ahistorical, yet these early chapters are still outside of the scope of his central thesis, which is to describe the history of the world from an Islamic perspective. This means that the true purpose of his book can only take shape when the timeline reaches the eighth century when Islam began to congeal as a power structure and when written records shape a more reliable historical narrative.

By 661, the Arabs seemed to have controlled an empire roughly the size that the Roman Empire had been during its apex. Such a rapid influx of wealth brought internal dissent with it. As different clans vied for control of the empire, prior to 661, three different men had been accepted as caliphs by the Umma. The third, Uthman, took a blade from a servant turned assassin and this brought about a succession crisis. Following this desire, two differing justifications for the control of the Islamic power structure emerged.

Those who wanted Mohammed's cousin and son-in-law, Ali, to be caliph made the claim that only relatives of Mohammed could rule. The members of another clan, the Umayyad, had once controlled Mecca and had waited long enough for a return to power. Who was or was not related to the Prophet made no difference to the Umayyad or their followers.

Ansary treats the ascension of Ali to the caliphate by veering his narrative into historical fiction:

> At first, Ali refused the honor; but every other prominent member of the Muslim community turned down the khalifate as well, and the rebels threatened to launch a reign of terror unless Medina chose someone they could live with and chose him fast, so leading Muslims crowded into the mosque and begged Ali to take charge.
>
> What a strange moment this must have been for Ali. For twenty-five agonizing years he must have felt like he was watching the ship drift off course. Three times, the Umma had rejected his leadership when he still would have had the power to make things right. Each time, he had been a good sport, because what else could he do? Trying

to seize the helm would have split the community. He had to choose between causing trouble or watching the enterprise falter; killing it or letting it die. (2010, 59)

This seems like a lot of introspection to assign to a character who possesses only the vaguest historical identity. An equivalent from Western history would be for a historian to try and interpret the thoughts of Archimedes before he was slaughtered by Roman forces at Syracuse during the Second Punic War. Plutarch, recounting tales he has heard from generations before his own existence, tells the readers that Archimedes was scribbling a math equation on the ground when he was himself erased by a soldier from the Roman Republic. Verifying the story is beyond the possibility of history, and so the story is more likely literature.

Regardless, Ansary still hasn't gotten to his central purpose yet, which is to tell an alternative history of the world through the perspective of Islam. The history of Islam in this era is well known and well documented by world historians (as volume 1 of this project will attest). It includes the Sunni-Shia divide of 661, the Umayyad Dynasty (661–750), and the intellectual heights of the Abbasid Dynasty's (750–1258) earliest years. Ansary chronicles this history, as he stated in his introduction, not by introducing any new historical research but merely by a narrative that had already been created by real historians.

At no time is a world historical approach in which the current subject of study is analyzed using analogies from other times and/or places ever applied. Consider this three-paragraph passage regarding the Buyid clan of Persia and their ascent at the Arabic court from advisers to de facto governors:

> These Persian viziers couldn't rule the rest of the empire, however, nor did they even care to. They were perfectly content to leave distant locales to the domination of whatever lord happened to have the most strength there. Major governors thus turned into minor kings, and Persian mini dynasties proliferated . . .
>
> You might think that training slaves to be killers, giving them weapons, and then stationing them outside your bedroom door would be such a bad idea that no one would ever do it, but in fact almost everyone did it in these parts: every little breakaway Persian kingdom had its own corps of Turkish mamluks guarding and eventually controlling its little Persian king.
>
> As if that were not enough, the empire as a whole was constantly fighting to keep whole tribes of Turkish nomads from crossing the frontier and wreaking havoc in the civilized world, just as the romans had struggled to keep the Germans at bay. At last the Turks grew too strong to suppress, both inside and outside the khalifate. In some of those little outlying kingdoms, mamluks killed their masters and founded their own dynasties. (2010, 123)

The Arabs and Persians used Turks as slave soldiers; by the 1050s the Turks took over as Islam's most dominant ethnic group. Eventually, the Turks repeated the pattern by creating a Janissary corps under the sultanate of Murad I around the year 1380. The policy, apparently, was driven by a dual purpose.

First, the Ottomans hoped to deprive the Orthodox Christian populations that dwelled in the Balkans of their young men, and this helped to prevent revolution. Second, this provided the sultan with an elite guard that existed largely outside of the family and ethnic politics that rotted the core of Ottoman government.

A world historical analysis of the Muslim slave soldier policies would reveal several parallels across time and place. Augustus established a praetorian guard made up of Germanic tribesman shortly after he became the Roman emperor. The guardsmen seem to have served him with fidelity, but after Augustus died the guard began to assert itself as a political force.

After the rule of Tiberius, Caligula was made emperor when he caught the favor of the guard and made into a corpse when he caught the ire of the guard. Claudius, he of the drool and stammer, was dragged into the position of emperor when members of the guard found him (wisely) hiding behind a curtain. His successor, Nero, was both chosen by the guard and forced into a grisly act of suicide (the old knife in the throat) by the Praetorians.

That list of Roman emperors made and killed by the Praetorian guard is long and speckled with blood, and the same pattern also asserted itself in Russia. In the exact middle of the sixteenth century, Ivan IV, or Ivan the Terrible, created the *streltsy* or "shooters" as a private guard to both engage in conventional war and to serve as a private guard. Russian society in the sixteenth and seventeenth centuries tended to be more conformist than those of either ancient Rome or the Abbasid Dynasty.

The *streltsy* did not revolt until 1682, when Czar Alexei of the Romanov family died and his brothers decided to make Peter Romanov, a ten year old, the czar over his feeble-minded older brother, Ivan V. The instigator of that revolt was Peter's older half-sister, Sophia. She wanted to rule by proxy and convinced the *streltsy* to rampage through the royal palace in Moscow.

Peter Romanov, eventually to be known as Peter the Great, witnessed the *streltsy* engage in a murderous purge. He survived only because of his lineage, but would carry his hatred of his own guardsman with him into manhood, when he would eventually use the power of the czar to bring the *streltsy* under his control.

Ansary does not engage in this kind of parallel historical analysis because he is renarrating a well-known history of the Islamic dynasties. His focus on the way that the Turks ascended in Islamic politics focuses on how the Turks waged campaigns of murders against their rivals:

> The Assassins were organized as the ultimate secret society. Out in the world, they gave no indication of their identity or their real beliefs. No one knew, therefore, how many Assassins there were or which of the people in the bazaar, or the mosque, or anywhere else was actually an Assassin. Recruits went through intensive indoctrination and training, but one accepted into the sect, each member had a rank reflecting his level of knowledge. Initiates moved from stage to stage as they presumably plumbed ever deeper levels of meaning in the Qu'ran, until they reached the foundation upon which all was built, whereupon they were admitted to the Sabbah's inner circle. (2010, 131)

This sounds like a plot sketch from *Game of Thrones*, or like a backstory associated with a video game. The assassins, like the Knights Templar, invented their own mystery. They were essentially just snipers of a sort, no different than any other groups of murderers who come and go across the history of empires.

Through the acts of stealth killing, they found they could control Islam's politics, and with it the money and power associated with the Abbasid Empire. These murders eventually destabilized the Abbasids and collapsed their defensive abilities. Ansary writes that, in 1092, after the killing of two major political figures,

> In the space of weeks [the assassins] had eliminated the two men most crucial to the shaky unity the empire enjoyed. These murders set off a debilitating power struggle among Seljuk sons, brothers, cousin, and relatives, as well as miscellaneous adventurers, a struggle that left the western portion of the empire in pieces. From Asia minor to the Sinai, practically every city ended up in the hands of a different prince—Jerusalem, Damascus, Aleppo, Antioch, Tripoli, Edessa—each was a de facto sovereign state owing only nominal fealty to the sultan in Baghdad. Each petty prince huddled over his possession like a dog over a bone and eyed all the other princes with suspicion. (2010, 132)

This passage reveals what Ansary might have done with a more modest approach to his topic. The Islamic response to the Crusades, and why the Crusaders proved capable of taking Jerusalem in 1099 despite the much commented upon superiority of Islamic culture and military prowess, is a legitimate historical topic. Ansary adequately explains how murderous internal politics in the Abassid capital weakened the ability of Muslims to defend themselves against a surprise outside threat.

Other historians have written of the "Arabic" or "Islamic" response to the Crusades, and Ansary may have wanted to avoid a well-established approach, or he may simply be hoping to have expanded the conceit to grander proportions. The failure of this approach again stems from a confusion regarding the traditional historical and world historical approaches. "What was the Islamic view of the Crusades?" is a good question for traditional historical research.

The question has a narrow purpose and clear boundaries for research; it cannot be expanded into a broader thesis such as "what was the Islamic view of world history?" because the question does not lend itself, as has been shown, to a genuine world historical approach.

When Ansary's book reaches the point of the Crusades, the most significant flaw in his tactic becomes visible. From the point of the Crusades onward, by necessity, Ansary must give a history of Western civilization because the Islamic world found itself in a state of near-constant reaction to the cultural and political forces that radiated outward from Christendom/Europe.

Prior to the Crusades, the Muslims had defined the boundaries of central Asia and dictated terms to their vanquished Christians and Jews who fell within those boundaries. The Crusades mark a change in the trajectory of history as the Christians now put pressure on Eastern empires.

In effect, the Crusades can be understood as connected to a world historical force that can be loosely called "militant Christianity." Militant Christianity should be considered one of the great shaping forces of European and world history, and it probably began with the king of the Franks and first Holy Roman Emperor, Charlemagne.

After his coronation in the year 800, Charlemagne forced a troublesome ethnic group, the Saxons, with whom he and the Franks had been warring for decades, to convert from a Germanic paganism to the more rightly guided version of Christianity propounded by the pope. By 804, Charlemagne and the Franks defeated the Saxons and murdered any Saxon who failed to convert.

For the next three centuries, militant Christianity remained an internal force in Christendom while relations between the Muslims and Christians could be described as downright cordial. Charlemagne traded gifts with the caliph of the Abbasid Dynasty, and the pope of the new millennium, Sylvester II (in office from 999–1003), greatly admired Islamic culture and mathematics.

Militant Christianity did not get turned into an outward forced until the mid-eleventh century, when the Turks took control of the Abbasid Dynasty. In 1071, when the Turks, led by Alp Arslan, defeated the Byzantines at the Battle of Manzikert, this gave militant Christianity a new and outward direction that manifested itself, for a time, in the four major outward crusades that took place between 1095 and 1206.

Ansary correctly notes that "the battle of Manzikert in 1071 CE, the one in which the Seljuk Turks crushed the Byzantines and took their emperor prisoner, came as stunning news. It also triggered a stream of messages from the Byzantines. The Byzantine emperors harangued the knights of the West to come to their aid in the name of Christian unity" (2010, 136).

But so-called Christian unity ceased to exist in the year 1054 when the Great Schism occurred between the Roman Catholic West where Rome ruled and the Greek Orthodox Byzantine East where Constantinople did. Pope Leo IX provoked his Eastern brethren by sending a cardinal named Humbert, at the head of a contingent, to Constantinople with a fistful of religious demands. Leo IX died while Humbert was en route, but the ambassadors from Rome presented their case to the Orthodox patriarch (a weaker Eastern parallel to the pope) Michael Cerularius.

The Western Christians demanded a series of reforms to the way the Eastern Christians worshipped. The Eastern Christians refused, and Cardinal Humbert excommunicated them on the authority of a dead pope. Cerularius excommunicated the Western Christians right back and, in effect, this defined everyone in Christendom as a heretic by at least someone's standards. This Christian history must be stated because the impulse behind the Crusades might have more to do with 1054 than 1071. From the Western point of view, saving Constantinople would be the equivalent of reuniting Christendom under the authority of the papacy and the Latin Church.

No mention of the Great Schism can be found in *Destiny Disrupted*, and that can be considered a flaw in the approach taken. By focusing purely on the Islamic interaction with the West prior to the Crusades, Ansary misses the most significant causal factors. By failing to study militant Christianity as a shaping factor, Ansary does not see that some explanation needs to be made regarding the sudden collapse of good relations between the Islamic world and Christendom.

Jerusalem's real importance for the papacy likely had more to do with its geographic location than it did as a spiritual destination. By securing Jerusalem for the Christian West, the papacy would drive back the Turks and create a secure region around Byzantium. This would bring all of Christendom together again under the military authority of the West.

Despite these omissions, the description of the Islamic response to the Crusaders or "Franks" (as the Muslims tended to call these warriors of the cross) is historically solid and narratively engaging. It is just hard to see how Ansary is taking a world historical approach to the topic. Over and over again, the internal divisions of the Turks led to the murder of any political figure who might call for a unified response to the Franks.

The Crusades and the forthcoming Mongol conquests, the latter of which Ansary calls the "Mongol Holocaust," are treated as connected under the chapter banner of "Havoc." The point being that, for the Islamic world, the Crusaders from the West and the Mongols from the East represented the dangers inherent with guarding regions of spiritual and actual wealth in the center of Eurasia. Ansary gives two years, Islamic and Western, when describing events:

> In 607 AH (1211 CE), Chengez's Mongols attacked China's decrepit old Sun Empire and cut through it like a knife into warm cheese. Seven years later, in 614 (1218 CE), the Mongols entered into the history of the Middle World. (2010, 151)

"Chengez" is Genghis Khan, and even though this book seeks to show the world from the perspective of Islam, the language is English and the framework is Western. The dates could have been adequately put into a timeline or appendix and the renaming of Genghis to "Chengez" seems like another unnecessary attempt at changing names for the sake of being different.

Again, nothing is explained here in terms of the causes of the Mongol rise in power. Genghis Khan has, like Mohammed, a mystical biography that was created after his death. Nothing supernatural is attributed to the Khan, but his biography in the form of "The Secret History of the Mongols" is not written until after his death. Ansary quotes from this spurious source again as if it was solid history: "Chengez's father was a chieftain among the Mongols but was murdered when Chengez was nine" (2010, 151).

In this, Ansary does not even get the mythology right. Genghis's father was, supposedly, a vagabond on the plains who stole Genghis's mother, Hoelun, on the night that she was married to another man. Temujin, as he was known before taking the title of Genghis Khan, was the son of a man who kidnapped and raped his mother. None of this may be true in the historical sense, but the fact that the Mongols told this kind of story about their origins reveals quite a lot about how they understood themselves.

As was the case with the Arabs before their seventh-century conquests, Mongol society, where horse riding, hunting, archery, and fighting were a part of daily life, possessed a military force that must have laid dormant for centuries. Something united the Mongols in the early thirteenth century, and that may or may not have been Genghis Khan.

More likely, the Mongols gradually coalesced into a singular military force as they found that raids into China became easier toward the end of the eleventh century as the Tang Dyansty declined. Later, when the Mongols encountered the "great men" mythologies of Christianity and Islam, this likely led them to create the mythological origins around Genghis Khan, or else the Khan was made up entirely of the bloody fantasies of later Mongol mythologists.

> Ansary is an amateur historian, and he occasionally evokes a cringe with statements like:
>> Some admiration has even accrued to Genghis Khan and his immediate successors based on the fact that they conducted mass-murder as a canny battle strategy and not out of sheer cruelty, destroying some cities utterly in order to make other cities give in without a fight. Read-

ing such analyses, one might almost suppose the Mongols did their best to avoid needless bloodshed! (2010, 160)

Genghis's "admirers" are not named, but one might assume that Ansary is referencing Jack Weatherford, whose book *Genghis Khan and the Making of the Modern World* (2005) sometimes borders on the apologetic. Yet Weatherford's brilliant book assumes that readers already familiar with the ghastly legacy of the Khan and his descendants will see his book as an addition to that narrative rather than a replacement. (Howard Zinn did something similar in 1989 with *A People's History of the United States*.)

Weatherford's book takes more of a world historical approach than does Ansary's because it takes a single time period, what might loosely be called the Era of the Khanate, and analyzes the period for global connections. The Mongols "made the modern world" by releasing Chinese technologies into Central Asia and the West, where those technologies would eventually make exploration across the Atlantic possible.

The collapse of the Islamic caliphate, in 1258, to Mongol conquerors created a conundrum for a religion whose truth was based in military conquest. Ansary is correct when he writes:

> The crisis was rooted in the fact that Muslim theologians and scholars, and indeed Muslims in general, had long felt that Islam's military success proved its revelations true. Well, if victory meant that the revelations were true, what did defeat mean? (2010, 160–61)

This could be the thesis of an entire book, and "What was Islam's response to military defeat?" would be a better traditional research question, but Ansary is not a scholar and no editor restrained him from stretching such a conceit into a "world history." Nonetheless, the most effective section of this book contains the reactions of shocked Islamic theologians to the Mongol conquest and slaughter.

Ansary notes that the Mamluk slave soldiers in Egypt stopped the Mongol advance into North Africa around the year 1260 and that, "Although the Mongols conquered the Islamic world in a roaring flash, the Muslims ended up reconquering the Mongols, not by taking territories through war, but by co-opting them through conversion" (2010, 157).

A broader historical analysis would indicate that the Mongols tended to be absorbed by local culture wherever they conquered. The Chinese also "converted" the Mongols in a way, when the Mongols found they needed bureaucracy and written language in order to administer a far-flung empire. Something similar happened to the Vikings in ninth- and tenth-century England as well.

Conquest takes a core people far from home, and once the blood dries, local customs and peoples tend to blend the differences between conqueror and conquered into meaninglessness. In retrospect, the Mongols could remain a coherent people for a limited amount of time. The fallacious premise that an Islamic "history of the world" can be narrated as a viable alternative to a world historical narrative centered on Western civilization is finally revealed with chapter 11, which is titled "Meanwhile in Europe: 1291–1600 CE."

The 1291 date corresponds with the retreat of the Christian Crusaders from the land of the Muslims and roughly corresponds with the time period in which the people of Christendom seized on the concept of innovation while also seizing the initiative in global exploration and trade. Much of what forced Christendom into a new and dominant phase had to do with technologies from the East and ideas from the Middle East. Ansary describes the typical conceit about how the Christian West advanced as a result of the transference of Islamic learning:

> The Arabic works found in Andalusia included a great deal of commentary by Muslim philosophers such as Ibn Sina (Avicenna to the Europeans) and Ibn Rush (Averroes). Their writings focused on reconciling Greek philosophy with Muslim revelations. Christians took no interest in that achievement, so they stripped away whatever Muslims had added to Aristotle and the others and set to work exploring how Greek philosophy could be reconciled with Christian revelations. Out of this struggle came the epic "scholastic" philosophies of thinkers such as Thomas Aquinas, Duns Scotus, and others. The Muslim connection to the ancient Greek works was erased from European cultural memory. (2010, 204)

Much can be debated about these statements: neither Avicenna nor Averroes worked all that hard to reconcile Greek philosophy with Islamic thought; both sided with reason when any conflict with Islamic theology made itself present during their studies. Averroes, in particular, argued that improbable religious teachings should be seen as allegorical. This is a nice way of saying that religious texts cannot be reconciled with reason and should be only occasionally taken seriously when the precepts line up with logic.

Ansary's statement includes almost no analysis and adds nothing to a well-known historical record. It could be that Islam's theological incoherency gave Aristotle's reasoning too little to conflict with. In the Christian world, the theologians who discovered Aristotelian logic held up traditional Christian teachings, based on Plato, to formal logical inquiry; this created a friction and then a fire. But Christianity made more claims that could be falsified through logical analysis and the study of probabilities than did Islam.

Traditional historical narratives connect this arrival of Aristotle's teachings in the West with the eventual development of the scientific revolution. A new analysis of the scientific method, *The Invention of Science: A New History of the Scientific Revolution* (2014), by David Wootton barely credits the Islamic scholars at all in the development of the West.

Instead, writes Wootton, the Columbian expeditions provided European intellectuals with a new set of analogies and a new vocabulary; words such as "discovery" and "facts" changed the European mindset. So too did the notion that things undiscovered could be found by looking out far enough, whether that was while sailing on a ship or by looking through a telescope.

At some point, it becomes clear that Ansary just does not understand the history that he writes about. In attempt to explain the development of European nation-states, he writes:

> A sense of shared peoplehood did, however, begin to develop over the course of the Hundred Years' War. For one thing, it became more distinctly the case that the people in France spoke French and the people in England spoke English. The French people began to feel ever more united with others who spoke their language and lived in the same invaded territory and ever more distinct from the English-speaking armies who kept coming amongst them. Meanwhile, English soldiers, thrown together with one another over long campaigns that might recapitulate a campaign their fathers had been on, and which their sons might go on, felt ever more united with each other in a team-spiriting kind of way. Over this period the "king" developed into something more than just the biggest of the nobleman: the idea of "kings" as an embodiment of "nation" began to form. (2010, 213)

None of this makes sense. English unity existed not at all, which is demonstrated by the fact that immediately after the Hundred Years' War ended the so-called Wars of the Roses (1455–1485), a civil war for the control of England, began. Wales, Ireland, Scotland, and England seemed disinclined to unite together or even to stop slaughtering one another because of their shared language.

The oncoming Protestant Reformation, in 1517, revealed the feudal fractions that existed in each region, and it could be stated that the English did not necessarily feel united as a "nation" in any conceivable sense until Queen Elizabeth summoned the winds to blow away the Spanish Armada in 1588. Soldiers fought for pay still, not so much for nation, and this is what facilitated most of the European fighting to begin with. Ansary's book at times devolves into semiliterate writing. Chapter 12 begins with:

> Between 1500 and 1800 CE, western Europeans sailed pretty much all over the world and colonized pretty much everything. In some lands, they simply took possession, entirely supplanting the original inhabitants: North America and Australia suffered this fate, ending up as virtual extensions of Europe. (2010, 217)

Such passages reveal the author's limitations but also provide a potential dilemma for a critic of his method. It might be argued that Ansary's approach to world historical studies failed less than he did. A better scholar, with a real understanding of global historical events, might do better than what this particular author did.

This would be to create a false separation between the author and the approach; the likeliest answer is that a more accomplished scholar would have realized that an "Islamic history of the world" is a failed endeavor and would never have begun writing it. This is the kind of book that would only be attempted by someone who failed to master the subject; poor writing comes along as a fellow traveler.

Why did the Ottoman Empire decline in relation to the West? The traditional answers are given regarding the military conservatism and insidious nepotism of the Janissary corps. Ansary does not mention that the Ottoman authorities banned the printing press in the late fifteenth century and then reiterated the ban with a death penalty in the early sixteenth century. The reiteration took place concurrently with the Protestant Reformation, and might be considered a crucial component for understanding the time period. None of this is included because no new concepts are included in this book.

Even the traditional history of the European and Islamic relations gets skewed. Of the 1857 sepoy rebellion, supposedly caused by the issuing of rifle-greasing cartridges made of pig and cow fat to Muslim and Hindu soldiers who worked for the British East India Company, gets a less than detailed explanation:

> One day a whole regiment of sepoys refused to load their guns. The officer in charge took decisive action: he put the whole lot of them in prison, whereupon riots exploded all over town. Apparently, it never occurred to the British that issuing bullet grease made of beef and pig fat might offend their sepoys. Their cluelessness reflected the cultural gulf between the British officers and their foot soldiers, a gulf that had not existed before Europeans arrived, even though Indian armies were frequently composed of many different ethnic and religious groups jammed together, Muslim Turks fighting alongside Muslim Persians fighting alongside Hindi-speaking Hindus and others. These groups quarreled and bristled at each other, but each knew who the others were: they interacted. (2010, 239)

This whole paragraph collapses when held up to the slightest amount of historical scrutiny. There is no evidence that the British ever actually issued the pig and cow fat cartridges. If they did, it's not clear how the sepoys would have known that this was the case. It could be that the rumor arose randomly, that it was based on total or partial truth, or that disaffected sepoys spread the rumor in an attempt cause a rebellion.

Also, while Britain's colonial venture into India is hard to justify in modern ethics, the British exploited divisions that they found but hardly created social division in the land of the caste system. Nor did the British conjure up the Hindu-Muslim animosity that existed for over a millennium before the East India Company arrived and which continues to make the Indian-Pakistani border a nuclear tinderbox.

Every chapter, though lacking in substance, seems laced with a bitterness toward the West. This in fact proves the point that an Islamic narrative of world historical events, even into the twentieth century, only demonstrates the irrelevance of Islamic theology (reform minded or terroristic) in the shaping of modern world events.

In particular, Ansary laments the devastation of the first Iraq war and the sanctions that followed in the aftermath: "After the war, the United Nations imposed sanction that virtually severed Iraq from the world and reduced Iraqi citizens from a European standard of living in 1990 to one that approached the most impoverished on Earth" (2010, 345–46).

This one sentence, by itself, reveals the full failure of Ansary's approach. The purpose of world history should be to create an explanatory narrative. Certainly, the postwar sanctions of Iraq can be criticized, but in a "world history?" The United Nations "imposed" sanctions, which indicates that power and momentum remained with the West (no one doubts that the sanctions emanated from US and Western leaders), and even the level of wealth that the Iraqis supposedly enjoyed in 1990 is compared to Europe. Clearly, the Islamic world has not been in control of its own destiny since the time of Napoleon, and so it's not clear why a supine region of the world should be at the core of any historical narrative.

At the end of the book, Ansary decides, strangely, to address the historical philosopher, Francis Fukuyama. This is a long passage, but must be quoted here to address Ansary's approach. Regarding the collapse of the Soviet Union (the cause of which is simplistically reduced to the 1979 Soviet invasion of Afghanistan), the author writes:

> In America, conservative historian Francis Fukuyama wrote that the collapse of the Soviet Union marked not just the end of the Cold War but the end of history: liberal capitalist democracy had won, no ideology could challenge it anymore, and nothing remained but a little cleanup work around the edged while all the world got on board the train headed for the only truth. In fact, he offered this thesis in a book titled *The End of History and the Last Man*.
>
> On the other side of the planet, however, jihadists and Wahhabis were drawing very different conclusions from all those thunderous events. In Iran, it seemed to them, Islam had brought down the Shah and driven out America. In Afghanistan, Muslims had not just beaten the Red Army but toppled the Soviet Union itself. Looking at all this, jihadists saw a pattern they thought they recognized. The First Community had defeated the two superpowers of its days, the Byzantine and Sassanid empires, simply by having God on its side. Modern Muslims also confronted two superpowers, and they had brought one of them down entirely. One down, one to go was how it looked to the jihadists and the Wahhabis. History coming to an end? Hardly! As these radicals saw it, history was just getting interesting. (2010, 346)

The title of Fukuyama's famous treatise gets mentioned by nonscholars much more than the book is actually read by them. Fukuyama's claims, as well as his world history, will be analyzed in this volume. It would require a book in itself to properly try to refute his thesis. *The End of History and the Last Man* (1992) is a serious book, and for Ansary to try and both mention the book and refute it in the last few paragraphs reveals something about the author's overall method.

What comes across in the paragraphs cited here is an exemplar of an Islamic scholarly mindset that one sees often in modern political discussions. This mindset is marked by the following: 1) a desire to be relevant, in any way, to global events occurring outside of the Islamic world; 2) self-aggrandizement well out of proportion with actual influence (Afghani Muslims did not bring down the Soviet Union; to say that this was the major causal factor would be to ignore Gorbachev's reforms, the failure of command economies, and the desire of ethnic communities for individual statehood, etc., which historians typically associate with the Soviet collapse); and 3) a passive-aggressive attitude toward terrorism (Islamic scholars might cringe at the violence of bombs exploding, but if it wasn't for terror and oil then the Islamic world would produce nothing at all of global consequence).

Here are some facts. The call to prayer comes down daily to the faithful in Tehran just as many times as it does in Washington, DC, which is to say not at all. The mosques of Iran are as empty as the dance clubs of Palestine, where hijab-less women in t-shirts dance to politically infused rap music, are full. Every February, Pakistan finds itself in a cultural crisis over Valentine's Day; the youth of the country like to buy each other flowers and chocolates, while the clerics scowl and whine about Western pollution.

It is not the case that the Middle East is overrun with refugees from France and Germany who are escaping internecine violence there, nor is the Western world being challenged by any form of thought that derives from Qu'ranic tradition. Ansary chooses to end his book with a short background of the terrorist movement that led to an attack on the Pentagon and World Trade Center Towers: "On that day, September 11, 2001, two world histories crashed together, and out of it came one certainty: Fukuyama was mistaken. History was not over" (2010, 347).

This final statement reveals that Ansary's approach eventually disintegrates into a wistful (hateful?) fantasy. Does Ansary really think that Fukuyama wrote that no historical events would ever happen again after 1991s Soviet collapse? Does Ansary think that the September 11 attacks really represented a challenge to Western cultural, economic, and military hegemony? Is he claiming Osama Bin Laden and his thugs as Muslims? This must be asked because Americans have been treated to one apologist after another who assures us that terrorism does not represent "true Islam."

Nothing of any intellectual or scholarly importance can be derived from *Destiny Disrupted*, but it should caution Western historian and intellectuals about the costs of degrading our own systems of values. Muslims and other apologists who complain (as they do incessantly) about the Israeli occupation of Palestine should be asked when the Muslims plan to give Istanbul or Egypt back to the Byzantines. Historical conquests are what they are; it's not possible to correct the consequences for past military conquests.

The concept of basic guaranteed freedoms, secular law, and free market economies are universally attractive ideas that just happened to develop in the West. These are not Western ideas that are imposed on other cultures through imperialistic powers. If Islam cannot reconcile with these values, then Islam's true destiny may be to die as a martyr for the world's Muslims.

TWO

The Silk Roads

A New History of the World

Peter Frankopan is a legitimate historian. This must be stated in the beginning because his approach to world history is framed in the same way that Ansary's was in *Destiny Disrupted*, only Frankopan writes with superior acumen and a greater level of analysis. Frankopan's book functions as a historical Potemkin's village, giving the impression of solidity but with not enough behind it to support his thesis. To be clear: world histories that veer eventually toward the special events that occurred in Western civilization cannot be invalidated through the notion of cultural bias. A world historical narrative must, by virtue of explanation, lean toward the West and the universal values that just happened to develop there. World history is about Western civilization in the same way that Shakespeare's *Hamlet* is about Hamlet; one must tell the story of the main character. If one tries to write a play about Polonius, one still has to tell the story of Hamlet in order to explain the connections, motivations, and fate of that character.

Ansary failed because his lack of scholarly background led him to attempt a narrative of world history that simply states a series of resentments; Frankopan's narrative does not necessarily fail, his history is too strong for that, but his ambition for the project and his skills as a scholar took him in two different directions. His ambition caused him to want to write a history of the world with a non-European orientation, but his skills as a scholar kept returning him to responsible history.

In writing style, Frankopan most closely resembles the monumental world historian J. M. Roberts, who crafted the best-read single volume history of the world. In fact, the creation of a single-volume history of the world forces a writer into a certain type of summative style, both of writing and of source citation.

The work of Roberts was analyzed in volume 1; he clearly focused his energies on the development of the West, and this was for the better. Roberts did not try to contort the narrative to focus on the East because, ultimately, it is constitutionalism and not Confucianism that dominates the current world. Narratives that focus eastward simply fail to go anywhere if the world historian's goal is to eventually connect history with the present.

Therefore Frankopan ends up telling a traditional and Western-leaning history of the world despite himself, and the disjunction between the book he told readers he wanted to write and the book he actually wrote demonstrates, more than anything else, that world history must feature the West as the protagonist.

As one might expect of a Byzantine scholar, Frankopan outlines his book in "themes" (the origin of the word comes from the way in which the Byzantine government arranged its political entities). He imposes the themes on the traditional chronological approach to world history and by doing so effectively establishes twenty-five chapters, each with the word "road" in the title. The repeated use of that word helps to keep a consistency in the narrative and fits well with the notion, stated by the author, that world history can be studied through different perspectives.

Because of this tactic, Frankopan's book cannot be effectively analyzed with a holistic approach only and must be critiqued by the thematic terms he develops and by the development of those themes behind his thesis. The overall effect of *The Silk Roads* is unsuccessful, but the history in the sections is effective. Frankopan's book thus provides world history, as a field, with an example of how a narrative of world history can be effective partially while failing holistically.

In the preface, Frankopan makes a personalized statement almost identical to Ansary's: an origin story about how a dissatisfaction with a particular narrative of history first made itself apparent in his psyche at a young age:

> For my fourteenth birthday my parents gave me a book by the anthropologist Eric World, which really lit the tinder. The accepted and lazy history of civilization, wrote Wolf, is one where "Ancient Greece begat Rome, Rome begat Christian Europe, Christian Europe begat the Renaissance, the Renaissance begat the Enlightenment, the Enlightenment political democracy and the industrial revolution. Industry crossed with democracy in turn yielded the United States, embodying the rights to life, liberty, and the pursuit of happiness." I immediately recognized that this was exactly the story I had been told: the mantra of the political, cultural and moral triumph of the west. But this account was flawed; there were alternative ways of looking at history—ones

that did not involve looking at the past from the perspective of the winners of recent history. (2015, xiii)

This whole passage, from the moment of adolescent inspiration to the lingering discontent with a Western-oriented vision of world history, seems to mimic Ansary's preface in *Destiny Disrupted*. The difference, again, is that Frankopan is a trained scholar and so his conceit that "there were alternative ways of looking at history" can be expected to contain a greater degree of scholarship. The problem is that Frankopan's scholarship is driven here by an agenda rather than by the facts. That there might be good reasons why the "winners of recent history" actually won, and the notion that it's a good thing they (we) won, does not seem to factor into his scholarly inspiration.

More importantly, Frankopan never states clearly what variation of world history to which he is trying to provide balance. As was the case with Ansary, Frankopan seems more disaffected by a "western civ. 101" tradition than he actually is by world history. This, as much as anything, is why this history of world history is needed.

H. G. Wells founded the field for the purpose of providing a balance to the history of Western civilization and even Will and Ariel Durant, who wrote almost exclusively about the West in their many volumes, began their history of civilization with a tomb about "Oriental Heritage."

The actual book does not reflect Frankopan's stated thesis. Chapter 1, "The Creation of the Silk Road," begins, as most histories of world civilization do, with Mesopotamia. The focus on Persia might give the impression that Frankopan's history will lean eastward, but by page five the narrative already, by necessity, turns to the Greeks:

> Greek commanders looked east with a combination of fear and respect, seeking to learn from the Persians' tactics on the battlefield and to adopt their technology. Authors like Aeschylus used successes against the Persians as a way of celebrating military prowess and of demonstrating the favour of the gods, commemorating heroic resistance to the attempted invasions of Greece in epic plays and literature.
>
> "I have come to Greece," says Dionysus in the opening lines of the Bacchae, from the "fabulously wealthy East," a place where Persia's plains are bathed in sunshine, where Bactria's towns are protected by walls, and where beautifully constructed towers look out over coastal regions. Asia and the East were the lands that Dionysus "set dancing" with the divine mysteries long before those of the Greeks. (2015, 5)

The only thing that Persia created of lasting significance to the to the world was military and economic pressure that seemed to facilitate the creativity of the Greeks. If that statement comes across as offensive in any way, please pause to consider the absurdity of a modern American being considered racist or ethnocentric for positive statements made about people on a different continent, with darker skin, who spoke a different language, well over two thousand years ago.

To praise the Greeks is not to insult the Persians, but very few cultures bequeath anything to the future (where is the great philosophy associated with the Habsburg Dynasty, or the mathematical achievement attributed to the Ottoman Empire?), and scholars should be grateful for what we do get without worrying about nonexistent biases.

After the passage on page five, Frankopan just keeps writing about the Greeks for several pages. It was, after all, Alexander who united Greece and Persia, not the Persian emperor Darius II. When the narrative does turn eastward, it is only to focus on China:

> The expansion of China saw a surge of interest in what lay beyond. Officials were commissioned to investigate and write reports about the regions beyond the mountains. One such account survives as the Shi Ji (Historical Records), written by Sima Qian, son of the imperial court's Grand Historian (Taishi), who continued to work on this account even after he had been disgraced and castrated for daring to defend an impetuous young general who had led troops to defeat. He carefully set out what he had been able to discover about the histories, economies, and armies of peoples in the Indus valley, Persia, and Central Asia. The kingdoms of Central Asia were weak, he noted, because of pressure from nomads displaced by Chinese forces who had turned their attention elsewhere. (2015, 12)

This is solid and scholarly history regarding China's Tacitus, Sima Qian, and his analyses of the Chinese geopolitical situation during the Han Dynasty. However, nothing is included in passage like this that is missing in any other respectable world historical narrative, even those that lean westward (see volume 1). Frankopan is not filling a gap or reorienting anyone's concept of world history, just retelling a well-known narrative in a single volume.

After the development of China's Silk Road is detailed, Frankopan returns to a history of Rome and the way in which Roman expansion gobbled up Egypt: "Rome had long cast a greedy eye over Egypt. It seized its chance when Queen Cleopatra became embroiled in a mass struggle for political mastery after the assassination of Julius Caesar" (2015, 15). Nothing about this narration leans away from the West. Caesar and the Romans are Latin and Cleopatra is a Greek queen of a Greek dynasty. The Egyptians themselves at this time could hardly be said to have a history that is anything but Mediterranean.

When the narrative turns away from the West, as it does in the following passage, Frankopan's historical narrative reflects the writing style that J. M. Roberts once applied to world history:

> Large-scale irrigation projects in the valleys of what are now Tajikistan and southern Uzbekistan built around the turn of the era show that this

period saw rising affluence and prosperity as well as increasingly vibrant cultural and commercial exchange. With wealthy local elites to turn to, it was not long before monastic centres became hives of activity and home to scholars who busied themselves compiling Buddhist texts, copying them and translating them into local languages, thereby making them available for wider and larger audiences. This too was part of the programme to spread the religion by making it more accessible. Commerce opened the door for faith to flow through. (2015, 31)

This type of writing, which excludes quotes from source material and avoids specifics such as the names of rulers and minor empires, etc., is typical of one-volume histories of the world. In this, Frankopan's writing resembles the aforementioned J. M. Roberts.

As was stated at the beginning of this chapter, Roberts wrote with a Western orientation and did not burden himself by trying to contort the world historical narrative to the East. Consider the language present in Frankopan's passage. Buddhism is called a religion and referred to as a faith. Buddhism is neither; instead it is a practice that is designed to help the practitioner attain a certain state of mind.

Practices such as Buddhism gained popularity in the East, but they called for a renunciation of the world and contained few teachings that can be refuted by logic and analysis. The Buddha was careful, as so many wise men were and are, of making statements that could be demonstrably refuted, and so the East never developed the kind of friction between logic and faith that eventually smolders into scientific fire.

In other words, Frankopan's narrative describes Uzbekistan, in this passage, but explains nothing in terms of why other areas of the world rather than Uzbekistan would create democracy and science. Otherwise, the reader is just learning about an Uzbeki irrigation system from two millennia ago, and this a topic would better fit normal historical, as opposed to world historical, methods of research.

Occasionally, Frankopan even works against his own thesis, as is the case when he writes, "When we think of the Silk Roads, it is tempting to think of the circulation always passing from east to west. In fact, there was a considerable interest and exchange passing in the other direction" before the quoting from a primary Chinese document in which Syrian goods and culture are praised.

In the previous chapter it was pointed out that Ansary failed to describe the conditions of North Africa and the Middle East in the late sixth and early seventh centuries in any sufficient detail. One cannot understand the Arabic conquests from 632 onward without knowing about the conditions of the time period.

For an apologist of Islam's history and precepts, a lack of knowledge about or misunderstanding of the time period might be necessary. If the time period was ordinary, then Islam must be extraordinary. However, if the time period was extraordinary, then Islam might be ordinary and indeed arbitrary as any idea that provided some level of military unification would have sufficed to conquer Byzantine and Persian territory.

Frankopan gets this history right and devotes a full nine pages to the situation in the Byzantine and Persian Empires as they existed just before the rise of Islam. This detailed explanation justifies the writing of his book, but, like Ansary, Frankopan shows too much respect for the mythologies of Islam and seeks to give undeserved historical credence to fanciful Islamic "histories." Take this paragraph:

> The rise of Islam took place in a world that had seen a hundred years of turmoil, dissent, and catastrophe. In 541, a century before the Prophet Muhammad began to receive a series of divine revelations, it was news of a different threat that spread panic through the Mediterranean. It moved like lightning, so fast that by the time panic set in, it was already too late. No one was spared. The scale of death was barely imaginable. According to one contemporary who lost most of his family, one city on the Egyptian border was wiped out: seven men and one ten-year-old boy were all who remained of a once bustling population; the doors of houses hung open, with no one to guard the gold, silver, and precious objects inside. Cities bore the brunt of the savage attacks, with 10,000 people being killed each day in Constantinople at one point in the mid-540's. It was not just the Roman Empire that suffered. Before long cities in the east were being ravaged too, as disaster spread along the communication and trade networks, devastating cities in Persian Mesopotamia and eventually reaching China. Bubonic plague brought catastrophe, despair, and death. (2015, 62)

Again, the tension in the narrative is between giving overmuch respect to Islamic traditions while stressing the importance of a sixth-century (typically called Justinian's Plague) contagion for causing the disruption of political institutions that gave rise to Arabic conquest and, later, the development of Islamic mythology and the conjuring up of a prophet named Mohammed. What does Frankopan mean when he writes, "a century before the Prophet Muhammed began to receive a series of divine revelations"? Is he speaking rhetorically as a way of keeping time (if so, it's only sixty-nine years before Mohammed first visited the cave outside of Mecca) or is he giving Mohammed's revelations the same historical veracity as he is the outbreak of Justinian's Plague?

The treatment of Mohammed in world histories amounts to one of the more fascinating changes wrought by the political correctness of the late twentieth and early twenty-first centuries. H. G. Wells and even the normally polite Will and Ariel Durant treated Mohammed as a charlatan, even as they paid respect to Islam as a coherent, if antiquated, political and social system that was good enough for the time.

Frankopan appears prepared to write of Mohammed as if the primary audience for his work were fundamentalist Muslims. This is likely not out of fear (Islamist thugs rarely read academic works and tend only to get riled up over material, like editorial cartoons, that doesn't require much intellectual processing) but as a form of hyper-respect to a people that are considered to be downtrodden and unfairly pressured by the West. Frankopan is signaling a sign of respect for Islamic culture, but this overcomes his logical faculties and creates the disjunction in his world history.

Again, if plagues and wars devastated North Africa and the Middle East, as Frankopan aptly notes that they did, then it would not have taken much to conquer the regions, and this makes the Arabic military successes of the seventh and eighth centuries less remarkable because these conquests provided the justification for Islam's "truth." To lessen the importance of the conquest is to lessen the importance of Islam as a shaper of history.

World historians must start treating the mythologies of all world religions in the same way that modern biologists and anthropologists treat Creationism. That is, as a mythology that persists despite the existence of modern forms of logic and science and, therefore, able to be dismissed.

Later, when writing of Mohammad's origin story, Frankopan compounds upon his earlier mistake by writing, "According to Islamic tradition, in 610 [Mohammad] began to receive a series of revelations from God. Muhammad heard a voice that commanded him to recite verses" (2015, 71). The phrase "According to Islamic tradition" allows Frankopan to show respect for the Islamic mythologies as if they were histories while at the same time allowing himself to maintain a respectable distance from the nonsense. He later writes, "A series of recitations followed over the coming years that were written down around the middle of the seventh century as a single text—known as the Qur'an" (2015, 71).

Of course, the more appropriate way to state this is that the Qur'an was made up entirely in the seventh century and attributed to a character named Mohammad who may or may not have existed. The conceit of the revelations themselves should receive no serious treatment as history at all, and to do so confuses the scope of the project and weaves itself, like junk DNA, into an otherwise necessary narration. "Although even establishing a secure sequence of events can be problematic, there is a wide acceptance that Muhammad was not the only figure in the Arabian peninsula in the early seventh century to talk about a single God, for there were other 'copycat prophets' who rose to prominence in precisely the period of the Perso-Roman wars" (2015, 71), the author writes. All the more reason to see the attribution of Islam to Mohammad as arbitrary. He, like Jesus, is mostly likely a composite figure constructed out of mythologies and forged by sudden political necessity.

Fortunately, the majority of Frankopan's structural problems become less noticeable after page one hundred. His book has a running theme regarding the word "roads." The word is included in each chapter heading. In the chapter titled "The Road of Furs," the reader learns this:

> The Khazars themselves did not adopt Islam, but they did take on new religious beliefs: in the middle of the ninth century, they decided to become Jewish. Envoys from Khazaria arrived in Constantinople around 860 and asked for preachers to be sent to explain the fundamentals of Christianity. "From time immemorial," they said, "we have known only one god [that is, Tengri], who rules over everything. . . . Now the Jews are urging us to accept their faith, promising us peace and many gifts." (2015, 107)

The ensuing narrative explains to the reader that the famous Byzantine missionary Cyril, who is usually paired with his brother Methodius in historical narratives, visited the khagan's imperial center and made an attempt to convert the Khazars to Christianity. Cyril, who might be the most successful Christian missionary in history, failed in this one instance as Judaism became the monotheism of choice instead. Frankopan later summarizes a letter from the Khazar ruler that explains the decision and the rationale that Judaism was "the religion of Abraham" (2015, 109). Here in Central Asia, Judaism found a new state that protected the faith with a military.

Etymology features effectively in much of Frankopan's narrative, such as in chapter 7, in which he writes that the Viking people known as the Rus (the progenitors of the Russian state eventually) made a living out of capturing and selling northern peoples into the coercive labor markets of the south. Of these people, "So many were captured that the very name of those taken captive—Slavs—became used for all those who had their freedom taken away: slaves" (2015, 114).

That particular fact was fairly well known, but the following excerpt reveals a linguistic connection that might not be:

> So widespread was slavery in the Mediterranean and the Arabic world that even today regular greetings reference human trafficking. All over Italy, when they meet, people say to each other, "schiavo," from a Venetian dialect. "Ciao," as it is more commonly spelt, does not mean "hello"; it means "I am your slave." (2015, 119)

Etymology might be underused by world historians. One cannot derive the context of a phrase such as "I am your slave," but its common usage as a greeting does indicate something about the ubiquitous state of coercive labor in the eighth century and beyond. Venice glittered in the historical sun, writes Frankopan, only because its geographic position allowed the Venetians to sell other human beings effectively into varied regions.

The trade in slaves facilitated economic changes, such as:

> In the eighth to tenth centuries, the base commodity for sale had been slaves. But as the economies of western and eastern Europe became more robust, galvanized by huge influxes of silver coinage from the Islamic world, towns grew and their populations swelled. And as they

did so, the levels of interaction intensified, which in turn led to the demand for monetization, that is to say, trade based on coinage—rather than, for example, on furs. (2015, 126)

Such a passage reveals the joy of world history as a discrete field. What were the major evolutions in world historical/economic development? Here, Frankopan argues that the slave trade itself drove the development of a money economy and that the speciation of specie occurred when coins took the place of furs.

The slaves came from the north, usually, where furs had value, but that value lessened as one moved to the sunnier climes of the Mediterranean and the Middle East. This passage also shows what Frankopan might have been able to do if he had not put pressure on himself to torture his narrative into leaning constantly away from the West.

Slavery, as an institution, also inaugurated the Turks into a new and militant Islamic force. Various Islamic rulers enticed or forced the nomadic Turks into fighting for the faith, "But as [the slave troops] began to be relied on increasingly not only in rank-and-file positions but in command positions, it was not long before the moment came when senior officers began to cast an eye on taking power for themselves" (2015, 127). The development of massive "slave" militaries, in which the commanders only imperceptibly bent the knee to their overlords, transformed the lands east of Baghdad, where the Abbasid caliphate resided, and created a new Turkish/Persian culture.

From that new culture, eventually the Seljuk Turks would seize control of Abbasid power and their military conquests into Byzantine territory would be the major cause of the Crusade. Too often, historians analyze slavery only through its ethical failings, but Frankopan understands slavery to be the central factor of eighth- and ninth-century society and that the economic, military, and political events of the time all branched from slavery's nexus point.

Because the Turkish victory over the Byzantine Empire at the Battle of Manzikert in 1071 is generally accepted as the major causal agent for the Crusades, "The Slave Road" is followed by a chapter about the Crusades. Frankopan's take, usually a safe one when dealing with human beings, is that plunder rather than piety inspired the Church to declare the need for holy war. The nobility desired to take Muslim territory and riches more than they did to control Jerusalem's temples and religion. The proof that supports this cynicism came after Saladin took Jerusalem in the Third Crusade:

> The fall of the city was a humiliating blow for the Christian world and a major setback for Europe's connections with the east. The papacy took the news badly—Urban III apparently dropped dead on hearing of the defeat of Hattin. His successor, Gregory VIII, led the soul-searching. The Holy city had fallen, he announced to the faithful, not only

because of "the sins of its inhabitants but also [because of] our own and those of the whole Christian people." The power of the Muslims was rising, he warned, and would advance unless it was checked. He urged that kings, princes, barons, and cities that were arguing with each other should set aside their differences and respond to what had happened. This was a frank admission that, for all the rhetoric about the knighthood being motivated by faith and piety, the reality was that self-interest, local rivalries and squabbling were the order of the day. Jerusalem had fallen, the Pope said because of the failure of the Christians to stand up for what they believed in. Sin and evil had overwhelmed them. (2015, 147)

One might protest that modern scholars cannot very well understand the motivations of people from the medieval era because the value systems of that prescientific and pre-Enlightenment era differed so much from the current time period. Yet Frankopan's analysis seems to be backed by the results of the Fourth Crusade, in which the knights of the cross stopped off in Constantinople and found that "a golden opportunity presented itself when one of the claimants to the throne in Byzantium offered to reward the army generously if they helped him take power in Constantinople" (2015, 149).

The Crusaders apparently decided too much time was required to get to Jerusalem and too much energy was required to conquer and keep it. Besides, the Greek Christians in Constantinople were technically heretics anyway and so the Crusaders conquered with such cruelty that

although they looked like men, the westerners behaved like animals, wrote one prominent Greek cleric mournfully, adding that the Byzantines were treated with abysmal cruelty as virgins were raped and innocent victims impaled. The sack of the city was so brutal that one modern scholar has written of a "lost generation" in the years that followed the Fourth Crusade as the Byzantine imperial apparatus was forced to regroup in Nicaea in Asia Minor. (2015, 151)

The Fourth Crusade provides a blood red point of connection between traditional Christian/Islamic histories and that of the rising Mongol armies to the northeast of Constantinople, and Frankopan ably exploits this connection by moving from chapter 8, "The Road to Heaven," to chapter 9, "The Road to Hell."

Unfortunately, the author employs the same historical analysis to the Mongols and Genghis Khan as he did to the Muslims and Mohammed. The biographical sources for the life of Temujin, or Genghis Khan, tend to be spurious at best, and their truth or lack thereof cannot be determined through using modern means of historical analysis. Yet Frankopan treats the narrative of Genghis Khan's life in the same way that he might recount the biography of Martin Luther, Napoleon, or Barack Obama. This is a fallacy because the veracity of the source material for the lives of each differs so much. Again, to treat history like this is to treat a statistical sample of three people in the same way that one treats a statistical sample of 2,300 people.

The "biography" of Genghis Khan should be treated similarly to Sergei Eisenstein's 1928 motion picture *October: Ten Days That Shook the World*. Eisenstein filmed actors involved in a loose recreation of "historical" events for the purpose of creating an origin story that served the purposes of the ruling Communist party. *October* must have enthralled illiterate Russian audiences from the twentieth century in the same way that the oral biography of Genghis Khan would once have done in the thirteenth and fourteenth centuries.

As is the case with Jesus and Mohammed, Genghis Khan may or may not have existed. Clearly *something* united the Mongolian tribes in the thirteenth century. Was it a single evil genius like Genghis Khan, or did random historical forces (such as the weather) force the Mongols off of the steppes and make their hunting lifestyle unsustainable so that, in its place, they had to join together and adapt their hunting skills to warfare?

Then, after having conquered territories in which "great men" mythologies were prevalent, did they feel the need to create a great man of their own? It feels safer to ask this question about Genghis than of the major religious figures of history, but this may only be because the Mongols brought no religious system of their own into the world.

This is a worthy question for a world historian: the Mongols in the thirteenth century are almost directly analogous to the Arabs in the seventh century in terms of lifestyle and military capability. Both the Arabs and the Mongols lived originally as horse- (or camel-, in the case of the Arabs) riding nomads. Their latent military skills, developed through hunting and the fighting of skirmishes, finally reached their potential when something united those discrete families into a military force. From horseback, both rapidly created massive land-based empires. Why, then, did the Muslims leave behind a religion while the Mongols did not?

With analogous reasoning, one usually begins by stating the similarities because doing so highlights the differences, and the differences help the world historian to pull out the deciding factors. The Arabs lived in and then conquered a North Africa and Central Asia where Judaism, Christianity, and Zoroastrianism dominated.

Judaism and Christianity centered on the concept of a single god, Christianity and Zoroastrianism both taught the existence of a heaven and hell, and all three were doctrinaire to some degree. This was the religious environment that Islam, as a tool of a new ruling (and male) elite, evolved in as a political institution. The nameless Arabic authors who dreamed up a Prophet Mohammed must have found inspiration in the Jewish and Christian founding myths that focused on important patriarchs.

The Mongols had little contact with the monotheistic religious traditions, and most of the Mongols worshiped (if the word is right) a vague sky god or engaged in other animistic superstitions. The Mongols defined themselves by ethnicity, and many converted to Islam without subverting their primary identity to the faith; Muslim Mongols still engaged in the invasion and subjugation of Muslim peoples.

By the time the "biography" of Genghis Khan was written, the Mongols needed an origin story that reflected the priorities of that moment; thus the creation of Genghis Khan. The story should be analyzed for its political and propaganda purposes, but it should no more be inserted as an actual history than is Eisenstein's *October*.

Frankopan has committed no personal scholarly sin, it's just that world historians work under the assumption that readers know how spurious the pre–printing press documents can be but write on with a "let the reader beware" attitude. This is a problem when writing for a more general audience, and it is also one of the reasons that meta-historical analysis tends to skip over the narratives in favor of broadly defined phases of history. Such an approach does not require the retelling of Muslim or Mongol origin stories, and "Big History" as a discipline evolves from that approach.

While the chapter titled "The Road to Hell" offers little that is new about the history of the Mongols, a two-page graphic in the middle of the chapter illustrates how the Mongol invasions and the Black Plague transferred around Eurasia. Death, riding on horseback, or wiggling around in fleas and sputum would not have it so good again until the discovery of the Americas.

The Mongol Empire itself, as stated before, morphed to fit the political needs of the Mongols at any given moment:

> The Ilkhanids seem to have been particularly adept at telling religious figures what they wanted to hear. Hulegu, for example, told one Armenian priest that he had been baptized when a child; the church in the west was so eager to believe this that illustrations were circulated in Europe depicting Hulegu as a Christian saint. Others, however, were told a different story. The Buddhists, for example, were assured that Hulegu followed the teachings leading to enlightenment. There were many instances of high-ranking figures in the Mongol world becoming Christian and then converting to Islam or vice versa, switching their religion as convenient. The phlegmatically faithful were masters at being all things to all people. (2015, 175)

This is more evidence that the Genghis Khan origin story should be viewed as a useful fiction. Nonetheless, the Mongol military and administrative apparatus clearly exists in full historical view, and it connected the eastern and western sections of Eurasia in a way that had not existed before. Goods, ideas, and viruses spread across the newly connected regions and, because everyone knew that the Mongols were in charge, relative peace facilitated the cultural exchange.

Chapter 10, "The Road of Death and Destruction," details the Black Plague's swathe across Eurasia and includes a biological analysis of the plague of the sort that has become common in world historical studies:

> Modern investigation into Yersinia pestis and plague has made clear the crucial role played by environmental factors to the enzootic cycles, where seemingly insignificant changes can transform the disease from being localized and containable to spreadable on a large scale. Small differentials in temperature and precipitation, for example, can dramatically change the reproductive cycles of fleas crucial to the development of the bacterium itself, as wells as the behavior of their rodent hosts. A recent study that assumed an increase of just one degree in temperature suggested that this could lead to a 50 per cent increase in plague prevalence in the great gerbil, the primary host rodent of the steppe environment. (2015, 183)

This use of modern experiments in biology to try and assign causation to a medieval pestilence is typical of the cross-disciplinary nature of world history as a field. The temperature in the fourteenth century was not, of course, rising. The Little Ice Age (credit goes to Brian Fagan for adding this feature of climate change to our understanding of the fourteenth century) encased Eurasia in icy winters, and summer downpours turned the soil into slop.

These conditions might have decreased the calorie intake of human beings (calories being crucial for immune strength and healthy breast milk) while increasing the number of creepy crawlies. This happened at a time when the Mongols had just connected Eurasia and when long winters forced humans into close quarters.

The Black Plague lacked the killing force that smallpox, or even the flu, later mustered against Native American societies. Even if the Black Plague festered 30 or even 50 percent of the Eurasian population into death, this would still be considerably less than the 90 percent of Native Americans who likely died between 1492 and 1900. Nonetheless, the Black Plague attracts more attention because it affected a literate people who left behind not just a chronicle of the Black Plague but, with it, a chronicle of their beliefs about the plague:

> In Damascus, wrote Ibn al-Wardi, the plague "sat like a king on a throne and swayed with power, killing daily one thousand or more and decimating the population." The roads between Cairo and Palestine were littered with the bodies of victims, while dogs tore at the corpses piled up against the walls of mosques in Bilbais. In the Asyut region of Upper Egypt meanwhile, the number of taxpayers fell from 6,000 before the Black Death to just 116—a fall of 98 per cent. (2015, 184)

The Syrian writer, using an analogy that is central to the Arabic poetic traditions, sees plague as "a king on a throne" rather than as the weapon of a celestial king on his throne. Death embodied its own purposes even as it disembodied the souls of medieval travelers. And the tax rates give accurate records of the number of deaths.

This is responsible historical writing that satisfies the aesthete and the accountant both. Medieval peoples, of all faiths, struggled to understand all that death through the prism of their superstitions. "Arabic handbooks written around 1350 provided guides for the Muslim faithful to do much the same, advising that saying a specific prayer eleven times would help, and that chanting verses relating to the life of Muhammad would provide protection from boils" (2015, 185).

One might wonder, if there is truth to the veracity of religious traditions, why such approaches produced no effect. Mumbo-jumbo affects a bacillus not at all except that it makes transmission easier when the faithful touch their heads to the ground or when the priests get coughed on by the dying during the reading of the last rites. Religion survived by reviving its oldest trick: the blaming of the victims.

> Avoid sex and "every fleshly lust with women," urged one priest in Sweden, and for that matter also do not bathe, and avoid the south wind—at least until lunch time. If this was a case of hoping for the best, then a counterpart in England was at least rather more direct: women should wear different clothes, urged one English priest, for their own sake, as well as that of everyone else. The outlandish and revealing outfits they had got used to sporting were simply asking for divine punishment. (2015, 185)

Is the greatest difference between the modern mind and the medieval mind simply that modern people understand the parameters of cause and effect better than our ancestors? Hunter-gatherers apparently did not connect that sexual intercourse was the causal agent for pregnancy. Why would they? It's possible to imagine that, after a certain age, everyone in the tribe became sexually active; there was probably no good reason to say that sex led to pregnancy any more than any other emergent adolescent trait (acne, hair growth, talking back to parents) did. Spirts from nature jumped into a woman's womb went the thinking.

Without biology, medieval people had no way of knowing the parameters of the Black Plague's causation. They worshiped a god who had dictated entire books that related His laws and pet peeves; *everything* seemed to piss Him off, and if one believed that sickness and misfortune were the manifestations of this god's wrath, then it became hard to pick out the main provocation.

A world, a mindset, agonized and died with the plague. It also may have created a generation of psychopaths; Timurlane (1336–1405), after all, would have been a child during the years of pestilential suffering. If people thought that a god sent the plague, then surely the act of slaughtering could be seen as a form of worship. Death must have been, to

Timurlane and his generation, what water is to fish. Frankopan focuses on the economic influences of conquest:

> Timur was not afraid to spend the money he extracted from the peoples he subjugated. He bought silks from China that were "the finest in the whole world," as well as musk, rubies, diamonds, rhubarb and other spices. Caravans of 800 camels at a time brought merchandise to Samarkand. Unlike some people—such as the inhabitants of Delhi, 100,000 of whom were executed when the city was taken—the Chinese did well from Timur. (2015, 192)

This type of authorial decision, in which it is assumed that the audience for the book knows already about how Timur's men soaked the soil of north India in blood but that we might not know of how this all gave China an economic boost, makes *The Silk Roads* well worth the reading, and if Frankopan had not overstretched his thesis, he might have written a traditional book of history regarding post-plague economics in central Asia and China and made it a classic.

Instead "The Road of Death and Destruction" reveals the last chapter that corresponds with the book's stated purpose and thesis. The Black Plague, coupled with climate change, was to erase one Eurasia picture and the Europeans were to draw a new one:

> Famine, unusual periods of drought coupled with the cases of destructive flooding in China tell a powerful story of the impact that environmental factors had on economic growth. Evidence from sulphate spikes in ice-cores from the northern and southern hemispheres suggest that the fifteenth century was a period of widespread volcanic activity. This triggered global cooling, with knock-on effects across the steppe world, where intensifying competition for food and water supplies heralded a period of dislocation, especially in the 1440's. All in all, the story of this period was one of stagnation, hard times and a brute struggle for survival. (2015, 194)

Not too long ago, the traditional take on the mid-fifteenth century was that it should be seen as the beginning of the European era. It was, but historians now note that no one would have known that at the time and that the mid-fifteenth century should be studied as a discrete time period. We should, in other words, pretend not to know that the Americas floated across the Atlantic.

From this paragraph until the end of the book, the historical narrative focuses, as it must, on Western civilization. The concluding paragraphs of chapter 10 would seem to run directly counter to the book's central thesis:

> Three ships set sail from Palos de Frontera in southern Spain on 3 August 1492, less than a month before the end of the world was being anticipated in Russia. As he unfurled his sails and set off into the unknown, little did Colon—more familiar as Christopher Columbus—

realise that he was about to do something remarkable: he was about to shift Europe's center of gravity from east to west.

When another small fleet under the command of Vasco da Gama set out from Lisbon five years later on another long voyage of discovery, rounding the southern tip of Africa to reach the Indian Ocean, the final pieces necessary for Europe's transformation fell into place. Suddenly, the continent was no longer the terminus, the end point of a series of Silk Roads; it was about to become the center of the world. (2015, 196)

The phrase "center of the world" may very well mean a literal geographic shift. Prior to Columbus, the Mediterranean was the center of the world, and control of that body of water fed the Alexandrian, Roman, Byzantine, Umayyad, Abbasid, and Ottoman Empires. When the Americas got added to the map, an entirely new Western Hemisphere became apparent and Europe now occupied the central space between the new world and the old.

At this point, less than halfway through the book, it becomes almost possible to essentially end this review of *The Silk Roads*. The book morphs into a traditional concise history of the world. Chapter 11, "The Road of Gold," details the Columbian destruction of the Caribbean peoples but does give a refreshing take on Columbus. Ever since the publication of James Loewen's 1995 book *Lies My Teacher Told Me: Everything Your American History Textbook Got Wrong*, a disdain for Columbus (and the day associated with him) has become a signal for liberal historical virtue. It is refreshing to read a narrative of Columbus that treats him as just another petty ship captain who was clothed in a little brief authority:

> Some of Columbus' men, infuriated by the way he obsessively managed every detail of his expeditions, by how stingily he rationed provisions and by how easily he lost his temper when anyone disagreed with him, returned to Europe with information that poured cold water over the admiral's reports, which were anyway becoming frankly tiring in their implausible optimism. Crossing the Atlantic was a farce, Pedro Margarit, a Spanish explorer, and Bernardo Buyl, a missionary monk, told the rulers of Spain: there was no gold, and they had found nothing to bring back other than naked Indians, fancy birds, and a few trinkets; the cost of the expeditions would never be recovered. (2015, 205)

This section reminds us that, while world historians deal with broad causes and effects and must often make large-scale conclusions about entire epochs, history is lived by ordinary individuals with bills to pay and day-to-day complaints. In the previous paragraph, Frankopan distills the most important moment in world history (the "discovery" of the Americas) to a group of disaffected workers who found a way to go over the boss's head and make a complaint.

That whole business about the discovery of a new world, with its long trip across the Atlantic made worse through its close proximity to a micromanaging jerk of a boss who is only interested in impressing *his* bosses at corporate, seemed less than worth the effort at the time. Historical causes are created in ordinary time and only become extraordinary with additional time.

Like chapter 10, chapter 11 ends with another teaser about the forthcoming rise of Europe: "although scholars have long called this period the Renaissance, this was no rebirth. Rather, it was a Naissance—a birth. For the first time in history, Europe lay at the heart of the world" (2015, 213).

Europe at the center of the world, Europe at the heart of the world. How is this a non-Western history of civilization? Chapter 12, "The Road of Silver," details the European exploitation of Latin American mines. Given the title of the chapter and Frankopan's interest in etymology, it is a bit surprising and even irksome that Frankopan does not include the fact that Argentina is named after silver's Latin name "argenti" (also the source of silver's periodic symbol of Ag), but he shows how New World precious metals funded the precocious desires of India's Mughal emperor Shah Jahan.

From chapter 13, "The Road to Northern Europe," on, *The Silk Roads* becomes about the world that Western Europe made. The first two sentences of that chapter, "The world was transformed by the discoveries of the 1490s. No longer on the sidelines of global affairs, Europe was becoming the world's engine" (2015, 236), indicate the shift. World historians frequently show signs of fatigue; for Will and Ariel Durant, this came in the form of excess verbiage, wandering narratives, and mislaid dates. Frankopan hyperventilates up some mixed metaphors and stumbles over clichés. His thesis is finished, but he continues on with the trek.

Militarism "prompted the rise of the west" (2015, 25), as the author puts it, while trying to counter the phantom argument that the Enlightenment caused Europe to move past the rest of the world. In fact, it has been understood for decades that the fractured nature of the West made innovation possible there and only there, as the rest of the world was governed by powers that were stale and stable.

Chapters 14 and 15, "The Road to Empire" and "The Road to Crisis," continue to explain the significance of Western Europe's power trajectory, and only passing references are made to the Ottoman Empire's sudden collapse. Too much (the Ottoman banning of the printing press, the resistance of the Janissary corps to new forms of military movement, the significance of Suleyman the Magnificent [1494–1566]) is left out here for this to be a book of alternative world historical perspectives. The "crisis" that chapter 15 details is simply the First World War.

In that chapter, Russia absorbs the narrative:

> Although a severe banking crisis in the late 1850s also played a role, it was defeat in the Crimea and shame at the terms that followed that

prompted the Tsar to abolish serfdom, a system under which a significant part of the population was tied to the land and indentured to wealthy landlords. Within five years, serfdom had been swept away, ending centuries of slavery in Russia. (282)

Comparing Russian emancipation to the ending of slavery in the United States, a process that occurred at about the same time, would be illuminating. At this point, however, the point of the narrative seems to be to crowd out facts that don't fit the chapter heading "road" gimmick. "The Road to War," chapter 16, offers only a summation of the traditional narrative, jazzed up with a little use of active verbs.

Gavril Princip's assassination of the Archduke Franz Ferdinand is describe thusly: "As the two bullets left the chamber of Princip's Browning revolver, Europe was a continent of empires. Italy, France, Austro-Hungary, Germany, Russia, Ottoman Turkey, Britain, Portugal, the Netherlands, even tiny Belgium. . . . Within a matter of years, gone were the emperors who had sailed on each other's yachts and appointed each other to the grand chivalric orders" (2015, 309).

World history, as a discipline, should offer something to the reader that traditional histories do not. The arrangement of traditional histories into categories based on a theme really does not fulfill this purpose, particularly when it would have been possible to give a short background to the events that took place in Europe while explaining what occurred in the rest of the world; this would have been unsatisfactory in terms of creating a sequential narrative structure but would have fit the stated purpose of the book more effectively.

Even chapter 17, "The Road of Black Gold," which details the switch of the world's primary energy source from coal to oil, is dependent upon the influence of the British navy. "Switching to oil would mean that the power and efficiency of the Royal Navy would be raised to 'a definitely higher level; better ships, better crews, higher forms of war power.' It meant, as Churchill noted, nothing less than the mastery of the seas was at stake" (2015, 321). The demand for oil meant that areas with natural reserves would be brought into the world economy, but on the supply side, which always falls into a pattern of creating industrialization, taxation, and the greater levels of prosperity on the demanding side.

Oil links "The Road of Black Gold" with "The Road to Compromise" (chapter 18), which redirects the narrative to the Middle East, where Britain hoped to establish a post–World War I level of economic control. Oil forms an important narrative link in this world history, but it is too thin to hold together a very big topic. Revolution seemed a real threat in the last years of the First World War, and the colonial powers that were, suddenly discredited by the act of ordering a generation to their slaughter in the trenches, worried that that the example set by Lenin and the Bolsheviks might be replicated by the colonized:

Complications arose when those who had seized power in Russia found their dreams of international revolution thwarted in Europe and so turned their attention to Asia. Trotsky, fizzing with enthusiasm as usual, took up with gusto the theme of cultivating the revolutionary project in the east. "The path to India might well be much easier to travel in the current circumstances and what is more, quicker than the one leading to a Soviet in Hungary," he wrote in a memorandum that was circulated to his peers in 1919. "The route to Paris and London is through the cities of Afghanistan, the Punjab and Bengal."

Delegates from "the enslaved popular masses of Persia, Armenia and Turkey," as well as from those of Mesopotamia, Syria, Arabia, and beyond, were summoned to a conference in Baku in 1920, where one of the principal Bolshevik demagogues did not mince his words. "We are now faced with the task of kindling a real holy war" against the west, he told listeners. . . . The hour had arrived, that is, for a showdown between east and west. (2015, 334)

Communism, in the year 1918, appeared as an ideology for the oppressed classes of the world. Marx's two grand categories, of the "oppressors and the oppressed," seemed to fit the colonizers and colonized just as well as it did the bourgeoisie and the proletariat. Frankopan includes a crucial moment in the previous paragraph, in which Communist ideology became symbiotic with anti-Western anger and in which it melded with the already downtrodden economies of the East.

The logic of Communism, once it was framed in East versus West terms, led the Soviets to the forced industrialization of the 1930s. This prepared the Russians and their empire for war against the Nazis but also destroyed the logic of Lenin's Communist International (Comintern), the stated aim of which was to spread Communist ideology to the globally oppressed.

Stalin focused on "socialism in one country" and therefore cut off the colonized masses from an ideology of violent revolution that might have appealed to the more militant sectors of the population. Socialist ideology, with its focus on class consciousness, would seem to have been an antidote to the divide and rule tactics used by the British and their colonizing counterparts.

After the Nazis went down in defeat, the Russians had no real ideology to oppose the West. Sputnik aside, the command economies of the East could not keep up with the West, nor did they really need to, except that propaganda demanded it. Frankopan includes the right moment but then fails to analyze its significance beyond the effect it immediately had on the British powers who worried over any revolutionary ideology that might interrupt their plans for control of the Middle East.

Still, "the compromise" of the title relates to the Middle East, its oil reserves, and the political structures complicated by the 1922 collapse of the Ottoman Empire and by the arrival of both Zionism and Zionists.

From oil, the narrative turns to crops and to chapter 19, "The Wheat Road." Here the narrative becomes irresponsible and reveals one of the problems with the writing of world history: it can stretch the ability of anyone to keep the facts straight.

Traditional historians work with specifics, such as submarine warfare or the impact of Spiro Agnew's vice presidency, and therefore rarely make specific factual errors. World historians stretch the boundaries of disciplines and are therefore more prone to mistakes.

Chapter 19 begins with the cutesy factoid that Hitler had been favorably mentioned in a British women's magazine. This is fine, as the Hitler industry has made it difficult to dig up any interesting entry point into the life and times of that little dictator. A paragraph about the Molotov-Ribbentrop (Soviet-Nazi) pact, however, that appears later in the chapter is a little more problematic:

> The idea of an alliance between the two states seemed beyond the realms of plausibility or reality. Since Hitler had been voted to power in 1933, relations between Germany and the USSR had deteriorated sharply, with vitriolic media campaigns in both countries portraying the other as demonic, ruthless, and dangerous. Trade had all but collapsed: while nearly 50 per cent of all imports to the Soviet Union had come from Germany in 1932, six years later the figure had fallen to below 5 per cent. But with the guarantees extended to Poland, the two countries finally had something in common: a wish to destroy the state that was sandwiched between them. (2015, 347)

Errors are pock marked throughout this paragraph. The Soviet Union was not a "state," it was a union composed of states under the dominance of a single party. Hitler was never "voted to power in 1933." He combined the office of chancellor (to which he had been inexplicably appointed in 1932 after having been trounced in that year's presidential elections) with the office of Reich president after President Hindenburg died. Then, having merged the offices, he issued a plebiscite to the German people. A plebiscite is not an election; a plebiscite is a dictatorial trick pulled for the purpose of hiding a dictatorship behind a thin sheet of democracy. Napoleon and Hitler both seized power and then let the people "decide" whether or not they could keep that power.

The purpose of pointing this out is not to nitpick the book or to shame the narrative with small factual errors. World historians are not specialists, so any individual portion of a world historical narrative then becomes susceptible to fact checking from traditional historical specialists. World historians should be careful in writing about events and citing facts because traditional specialists who read world histories can (and will) dismiss the entire enterprise of world history as academically unserious.

Structurally, the problem with "The Wheat Road" is Frankopan's thesis that the Germans desired Russian land because of the rich wheat fields that grew in Russia's black soil. "Over the course of the second half of 1940 and early 1941, it was not just the military who were to work on the logistics of invasion, but economic planners too. They were led by Herbert Backe, an agricultural specialist" (2015, 357). Was the primary reason for the Nazi invasion of the USSR really to secure the wheat fields of Russia? This lengthy paragraph would indicate that:

> Agriculture in southern Russia and Ukraine had grown at a ferocious speed before the 1917 Revolution, boosted by growing domestic demand, rising exports and scientific research into the best-quality wheat and how to maximise yields from lands that had been grazed for millennia by nomads and their livestock. No one knew the potential of the steppes, which had expanded production so quickly in the late nineteenth and early twentieth centuries, better than Herbert Backe: his area of expertise, and the topic of his doctoral dissertation, was Russian grain. . . . As he stressed to Hitler, Ukraine was the key: control of the rich agricultural plains that ran across the north of the Black Sea and on past the Caspian would "liberate us from every economic pressure." Germany would be "invincible" if it could take the parts of the Soviet Union that held "immense riches." Gone would be the dependence on the USSR's goodwill and its whimsical leadership; the effects of the British blockade of the Mediterranean and the North Sea would be massively reduced. This was the chance to provide Germany with access to all the resources it needed. (2015, 359)

Again, the decision to use the "roads" concept seems to have led Frankopan to search for connections that will fit under that conceit. Historical narratives should develop naturally from the study of the facts. The desire to control the wheat fields of Russia certainly featured in the Nazi plans to invade the Soviets, but it was not a primary reason. World history has been troubled by commodity historians who seek to take an item (really any item will do) and trace its connections to various civilizations and time periods. By focusing on wheat as a connecting factor, Frankopan has absorbed and shrunken this approach for chapter 19.

"The Road to Genocide," chapter 20, focuses on the Holocaust and its eventual effect on the Middle East, and this sets up further chapters about the rise of America, the Cold War, and the way in which the creation of Israel destabilized the Middle East. These chapters not only fail to align with the thesis of a non-Western history of the world, but they also seek to twist the narrative toward a specific and flawed conclusion: Frankopan, like Ansary, wants to end his book with the September 11, 2001, terrorist attacks:

> Two thousand nine hundred and seventy-seven people died on 9/11, along with nineteen terrorists. The psychological impact of the attacks, which saw the collapse of both of the Twin Towers and the Pentagon

building damaged, was intense. Terrorist acts committed against embassy buildings or American troops abroad were shocking enough, but a co-ordinated attack against mainland targets was devastating. The haunting and terrifying footage of planes being deliberately flown into buildings, and the scenes of disaster, chaos, and tragedy that occurred in the aftermath demanded an immediate and epic response. (2015, 482)

Then president G. W. Bush possessed a level of idiocy paralleled only by Kaiser Wilhelm II. That Bush happened to be in power at a time of national crisis is the real tragedy of 9/11, as his presidency committed the same kind of crimes in the Middle East that Al-Qaeda committed in the United States, only at a greater scale.

The 9/11 terrorist attacks are not the return of history, but they should also not be the concluding section of a world history. The attacks themselves, occurring almost a decade after the collapse of the Soviet Union, would not have been much more than a temporary tragedy in the news like the *Challenger* explosion, the Columbine killings, or the Soviet Chernobyl meltdown had they not proved concurrent with a president and administration that made decisions without any intellectual engagement or knowledge at all of world events.

Bush seemed to know only one thing about history, and that was a vague knowledge of Britain's role in World War II, and so his inexplicable decision to invade Iraq was loosely based, again inexplicably, on the idea that he did not want to invoke appeasement as an international strategy. Bush's "Road to the White House" proved more decisive for world history than Bin Laden's "Road to Tragedy" (Frankopan's final chapter), and Bush's idiocy proved more destructive to the Middle East than Bin Laden's psychopathy was for the United States. But to understand that, one would have to abandon the conceit that world history can be told with a non-Western perspective, which is not what Frankopan set out to do.

THREE
A People's History of the World

In 1980, *A People's History of the United States* by Howard Zinn was published and became the rare book of history that managed to settle into the bones of American culture. Zinn's thesis, which must have been derived and written during the cultural shifts that occurred in the 1960s and 1970s, was that the traditional narrative of US history focused so much on the elite classes that they almost amounted to conservative propaganda. The history of the "people," meaning the underclass, the leftists (genuine fight the power leftists, not the coffeehouse liberals who chide people for assuming someone's gender), still needed to be written. Zinn's book aptly filled that gap and was an important addition to the historiography of the United States. Can the same "people's history" approach be applied to world history? Chris Harman makes the attempt in his *A People's History of the World: From the Stone Age to the New Millennium* (1999).

Before exploring these books, one question should be asked (and addressed) and two points should be made about the notion of a "Marxist" history of the world, which both of these books proclaim to represent. First, the question: Is an attempt to understand history through a Marxist perspective somehow more intellectually respectable than making an attempt to understand the human psyche through a Freudian perspective? Or, phrased differently, should Marx be taken more seriously than anyone else in the nineteenth-century pantheon of big thinkers?

The answer to that is "yes." Marx has more to say to the modern historian than Freud has to say to the modern psychologist because Marx was more careful in his connecting of theory to the source material of history than Freud was in connecting his theory to the source material of the human psyche. This leads to the two points that should be made.

1. The capitalism versus communism "debate" that animates so much of the conservative political discourse is based on false prin-

ciples. One cannot, for example, say that "Communism is a failure" because one cannot separate all the factors between two societies so that capitalism, by itself, stands in opposition to communism by itself. It could be that *any* economic/political system would work passably well when combined with abundant natural resources, the Haber process, and cheap and effective means of birth control. It's not possible to disaggregate economic systems from other political and historical factors so that they can be set against each other. For example, would the United States have "won" the Cold War if the United States had suffered from the wreckage of its infrastructure and lost twenty-seven million people as a result of a Nazi invasion? Also, it could be, for example, that Russian historical circumstances made it so that *any* political or economic system would likely fail in comparison with other areas of the world where the circumstances were more favorable to a better standard of living. Free market capitalism, when infused into Russia after 1991, did not have the effect of normalizing the Russian political system.
2. No modern socialist or communist thinker so far has answered the question of "what's so wrong with economic inequality?" The word "inequality" cannot function like the word "murder," in which the connotation is always negative. Capitalism creates a class of superrich, but the existence of this class might also create conditions by which the bottom economic classes can still enjoy luxuries like clean running water, cable television, healthy food (in the sense that it's not rotten or infected), and in-house refrigerators. What makes a greater level of income equality superior to income inequality?

Marxism is intimate with history, and it is a theory of exploitation and power that derives from genuine historical circumstances that derived largely after the eighteenth-century industrial revolution. Marxist historians, including Zinn, argue that history from about 1750 to the present can be understood through the framework of economic exploitation and class struggle.

Marx clearly believed that the totality of human history in civilization was the pitting of an exploitative class against an exploited class. That analogy can be stretched too far: Are women an exploited class? Are all people of color? Are we now in an era in which wealthy countries can be thought of as an entire class of exploiters and in which the exploited now exist in the developing world? Or, and this is the question at hand here, can the notion of class exploitation be expanded back into the origins of human civilization and succeed as a core explanatory thesis for world history?

No, it cannot, if only because it does the entire subject of world history a disservice to relegate it to an argument on behalf of a modern political ideology. Yet, precisely because Marxism was created from the raw material of history, a Marxist must be as fluent in history as a physicist is in calculus. The "world history" offered by Harman shows little evidence of such fluency, and this harms his thesis.

Harman's book was published in 1999, which means (mercifully) that the reader will not be subjected to watching historical facts be tortured into a concluding chapter on the 9/11 attacks. Harman, like all of the historians and political scientists of the West, were still trying to make sense of the 1991 Soviet collapse and still trying to find a means to counter Francis Fukuyama's provocation that history had ended. This notion was very much on Harman's mind from the very beginning:

> An adviser to the US State Department, Francis Fukuyama, received international acclaim when he spelt out this message in 1990. We were witnessing no less than "the end of history," he declared in an article that was reproduced in scores of languages in newspapers right across the world. Great social conflicts and great ideological struggles were a thing of the past—and a thousand newspaper editors and television presenters agreed. (2018, v)

This is followed, a paragraph later, by this curious assertion:

> Capitalism as a way of organizing the whole production of a country is barely three or four centuries old. As a way of organizing the whole production of the world, it is at most 150 years old. Industrial capitalism, with its huge conurbations, widespread literacy and universal dependence on markets, has only taken off in vast tracts of the globe in the last 50 years. (2018, v)

What is Marxism? Is it a revolutionary ideology that was born in reaction to capitalism, or is it a sociological framework for understanding the entirety of human history? Marx himself never quite answered the question, and his notion that history could be viewed as a struggle between classes (of which the bourgeoisie and proletariat were only the most modern variation) was never given sufficient historical support. The *Communist Manifesto* includes this phrase, only as a framework for history:

> The history of all hitherto existing society (b) is the history of class struggles. Freeman and slave, patrician and plebeian, lord and serf, guild-master (c) and journeyman, in a word, oppressor and oppressed, stood in constant opposition to one another, carried on an uninterrupted, now hidden, now open fight, a fight that each time ended, either in a revolutionary re-constitution of society at large, or in the common ruin of the contending classes. In the earlier epochs of history, we find almost everywhere a complicated arrangement of society into various orders, a manifold gradation of social rank.

> In ancient Rome we have patricians, knights, plebeians, slaves; in the middle ages, feudal lords, vassals, guild-masters, journeymen, apprentices, serfs; in almost all of these classes, again, subordinate gradations. The modern bourgeois society that has sprouted from the ruins of feudal society, has not done away with class antagonisms. It has but established new classes, new conditions of oppression, new forms of struggle in place of the old ones. (14)

Here Marx committed a simple sampling error. His historical conclusions about society being conceived of "oppressors and oppressed" are based only on the history of Western Europe. How would Marx have incorporated, say, the history of Australian and Tasmanian aboriginals who still lived in hunter-gatherer societies into his sociological/historical framework? In addition to a sample error, Marx's categories are too broad. Think of a proletarian woman living in late eighteenth-century England who is married to an abusive husband; she is oppressed by the oppressed but does this make her a revolutionary class unto herself?

This latter point is crucial because Marxist historians, by and large, have never dealt well with women's rights as an issue, except to vaguely proclaim female working-class equality, and by ignoring women as a special historical category these historians actually miss the real revolutions that have reworked society since industrialization.

Harman is in a hurry to get away from these questions and to the eighteenth century in his world history so that his Marxist sociological framework will make more sense. One more point must be made before reviewing Harman's Marxist approach to world history: Because Marxism is by definition anti-capitalist, and because capitalism is the world's dominant system, the Marxist must believe that something is profoundly wrong with the world as it is.

In 1992, Francis Fukuyama positioned himself as the bearer of good news, and Harman was as distressed by this as any other historian with a social change agenda. After including the obligatory assumption that the twentieth century ranks as the worst in human civilization: "History has not ended," wrote Harman, "and the need to understand its main features is a great as ever. I have written this book in the hope that it will aid some people in this understanding (2018, vi).

The modern version of Fukuyama, divorced of the political science, is Steven Pinker, whose 2012 classic *The Better Angels of Our Nature* made the case that life is now better than ever. Critics of Fukuyama and Pinker need to actually engage with those works, not dismiss them with vague authorial asides, but that is another subject for another time.

If capitalism should be blamed for the world's problems, and if there is hope for a better world after capitalism, then there must have once been a better human society before capitalism. It's incumbent upon Marxists to assert this because if capitalism is a corrupting influence, then it must have something pristine to corrupt. The prologue includes the heading "Before Class," and includes this ghoulish decree: "The world as we enter the 21st century is one of greed, of gross inequalities between rich and poor, of racist and national chauvinist prejudice, of barbarous practices and horrific wars" (2018, 3).

Hunter-gatherer societies shared resources and would not tolerate the development of elite classes; a sparse bit of evidence and a few quotes from scholars and Jesuits is used to back this claim and to refute the notion that humans in hunter-gatherer societies tended to murder each other at the slightest provocation. In his book *The World Until Yesterday: What Can We Learn from Traditional Societies?* Jared Diamond observed that in 2006 he could stand in an airport in New Guinea with people of different New Guinean ethnic and tribal backgrounds, something "that would have been unimaginable in 1931, when encounters with strangers were rare, dangerous, and likely to turn violent" (2012, 4). Hunter-gatherer societies might be egalitarian for the intratribal members but tended to treat individuals outside the tribe with hostility.

Both of Harman's assertions, the gloomy one about the current state of the world and the optimistic one about the precapitalist nature of humanity, have failed a more scientific test of evaluation. Pinker's 2012 *Better Angels* provided proof to the contrary. Yet Harman does not write like a fool, as this paragraph indicates:

> Under hunting and gathering, the need to carry children on the daily round of gathering and on the periodic moves of the whole camp had led to very low birth rates. Women could not afford to have more than one child who required carrying at a time, so births were spaced every three or four years (if necessary through sexual abstention, abortion, or infanticide). (2018, 13)

Killing an infant would seem to be a desperate step made by desperate people, and one can easily imagine that if a rash of infanticide affected a poor and modern urban community, that capitalism's evils might be invoked.

The transition into civilization gets the basic treatment; food surpluses created a settled lifestyle and class divisions. Although the book was published in 1999, well into the era when world historians understood disease transmission and the role that animal domestication played in it to be one of the defining factors of world civilization, Harman mentions this not at all. His focus is on the development of class divisions, which happens to be the title of chapter 3. Civilization led to property, and this became the basis for exploitation: the ruling class expropriated land and took slaves. The two most important paragraphs of his book explain the ideological underpinning of his approach:

> Why did people who had not previously exploited and oppressed others suddenly start doing so, and why did the rest of society put up with this new exploitation and oppression? The record of hundreds of thou-

sands of years of hunter-gatherer society and thousands of years of agricultural society show that "human nature" does not automatically lead to such behavior.

The only account of human society which comes to terms with the change is outlined by Karl Marx in the 1840s and 1850s and further elaborated by Frederick Engels. Marx put the stress on the interaction between the development of "relations of production" and "forces of production"/Human beings find new ways of producing the necessities of life, ways that seem likely to ease material problems. But these new ways of producing begin to create new relations between members of the group. At a certain point they either have to embrace the new ways of relating to each other or reject the new ways of making a livelihood. (2018, 24)

This assertion about hunter-gatherer societies leads to a false form of reasoning. Precivilized societies are both egalitarian to insiders and hyperviolent to outsiders; postcivilization societies tended to have internal oppression but could incorporate "outsiders" into political institutions with relatively less violence per capita.

What is curious about the Marxist perspective is that Harman clearly understands that "natural catastrophes, exhaustion of the land and wars could create conditions of acute crisis in a non-class agricultural society, making it difficult for the old order to continue" (2018, 25), yet he doesn't see how capitalism leads to improved agricultural production and the modern marvel that is a supermarket.

If the force that drives human civilization is class conflict, then why aren't there major wars between the ruling classes? The peasants of one empire or country have never declared war on one another. Harman declares that "in much of Eurasia and Africa private property was to develop among both the ruling class and the peasantry, but only over many centuries, with deep splits within ruling classes, bloody wars and sharp conflicts between exploited and exploiting classes" (2018, 28).

Such analysis ignores other factors, such as a lack of rapid communications systems, that might cause international conflicts. Also, both the Byzantine and Ottoman Empires operated largely through bureaucratic control of the economy, and the Incas in Peru had no private property at all. Yet each of those political entities contained class divisions and often gruesome forms of oppression.

As was mentioned earlier, the status of women in the Marxist worldview has always been complicated, but Harman does address the issue with chapter 4, "Women's Oppression." Harman explains how: "Gathering, the main source of nutrition for hunter-gatherer societies, had been fully compatible with childbearing and breastfeeding" (2018, 29).

The development of agriculture based on muscle power and plows gave men a sudden new power in society and the household. While it is certain that the status of women in hunter-gatherer societies was better than in civilization, Harman's reference to those societies as "primitive communism" is a bit much.

Still, there is something to the thesis that civilization brought with it a new form of exploitation, and Harman claims that in ancient Egypt, "The growth in the power and wealth of the ruling class drove the living standards of the mass of people down to the minimum necessary for survival—and sometimes even lower" (2018, 33). The monumental architecture that features so prominently in Egypt's history came about as a result of the labor of the lower classes.

The rulers, partially kept in place with a scam theology, came to power by marshaling the labor of other peoples, but eventually would harden into inflexible bureaucracies. Harman returns to Marx to explain this:

> As Marx noted in the Communist Manifesto, class struggles historically could end "either in a revolutionary reconstitution of society at large, or in the mutual ruin of the contending classes."
>
> These cases confirm his account. A ruling class which once played a part in developing the "forces of production" did indeed become a fetter on their subsequent growth, leading society as a whole into a period of social upheaval. (2018, 39)

At this point, Harman's world history begins to suffer from its lack of comprehensiveness. Part 2, "The Ancient World," arrives at only page 42. Only a few words are spent explaining that "there were societies across wide swathes of Eurasia and Africa which began to make use of the technological advances of the 'urban revolution'" (2018, 45), but the focus of part 2 is on the Greek, Roman, and Christian connection.

Small sections on Indian and Chinese history do precede these parts, but they seem not to fit Harman's central thesis and sit uneasily in his book. India's whole culture, from its politics to its religion, embraced inequality and did so without a modern variation of capitalism. Brahmins and Untouchables were not included in Marx's categories of oppressors and oppressed. Harman just writes a traditional history of the region without really trying to incorporate his Marxist thesis.

The chapter on China includes this interesting paragraph:

> The German-American historian of China, Karl Wittfogel, argued, while still a Marxist in the 1930s, that there were similarities between China in this period and Europe during the later stages of feudalism almost 2,000 years later. China could have been transformed by the merchant "bourgeoisie" into a new society based overwhelmingly on production by wage laborers for the market. Instead, it fell under the dominance of the bureaucracy of the state, which succeeded in channeling the surplus away from both the merchants and the old aristocracy and concentrating it in its own hands. The merchants supported the state in its struggle against the aristocracy, only to see themselves robbed of the fruits of victory by the state bureaucracy. (2018, 57)

Trade never exactly dissolved in China, but Confucianism did not favor the merchant classes, and the Confucians saw merchants only as middlemen who did no work but only added cost to the price of purchase. The lowly status of the merchant class, and the fact that China's Confucian elite represented the only bureaucracy in Asia that was well educated and largely well meaning, made it a certainty that the court advisors would claim power.

Again, though, this Confucian dominance creates a problem for the Marxist view of history. Confucianism would, eventually, lead to Neo-Confucianism by the tenth century. Neo-Confucianism evolved into one of the most oppressive state ideologies in all of human history, as the culture of the Chinese court and upper-class society sanctioned the process of foot binding for upper-class women. Peasant women, who had to work in the fields, were spared this act of social and physical crippling. Outsiders (even the Mongols) expressed abhorrence at the process. Speaking of the Chinese working class, Harman includes this curious statement:

> The peasants could not establish a permanent, centralized organization capable of imposing their own goals on society. Their livelihood came from farming their individual plots and they could not afford to leave them for more than a short period of time. Those who did so became non-peasants, dependent upon pillage or bribes for their survival, open to influence from whoever would pay them. Those who stayed on their land might dream of a better world, without toil, hardship and famine. But they depended on the state administrators when it came to irrigation and flood control, the provision of iron tolls, and access to goods which they could not grow themselves. They could conceive of a world in which the administrators behaved better and the landowners did not squeeze them. But they could not conceive of a completely different society run by themselves. (2018, 61)

This sounds like a Leninist explanation for why peasants don't automatically revolt. Lenin wrote that the peasants aren't ideologically ready for revolution, so what is to be done? Lenin, and later Mao, made the peasants a revolutionary class, but one that was too ignorant for revolution, so therefore they must be directed by Communist intellectuals.

Harman is right that peasants cannot coalesce around a political ideal; peasants lack education and that makes political ideals just as inaccessible as calculus to them. The immediate logical alternative, then, is to have the revolution led by intellectuals who do have access to revolutionary ideals, yet that is what created the Communist bureaucracies and police states in the lands of the peoples' wills.

Greece and Rome, the ancestors of the West and therefore of capitalism Marxism fit the thesis of history as being driven by upper-class exploitation more closely. Haram writes of the "struggle between the rich landowners, who farmed their land with relatively large numbers of slaves while keeping well clear of anything approaching manual labor themselves, and the mass of smaller farmers and artisans" (2018, 66). In Greece, the historian can see the early history of lower-class resentment, especially in Athens, where "the pressure from below resulted in even more radical changes—the replacement of both oligarchy and tyranny by 'democracy'" (2018, 67).

Statements such as, "The Greek city states, unencumbered by the gross bureaucracies of the Mesopotamian, Assyrian, and Persian empires, were able to show a greater dynamism and to command the active allegiance of a much greater proportion of their populations when it came to war. This explains the ability of the combined Greek states to hold back invading armies early in the 5th century BC" (2018, 69) remind the reader that Harman's Communism is not synonymous with the hideous statist structures represented by the Soviet block or Mao's China.

Bureaucracy develops as a way to protect power and property and also to ensure accountability. It's never been clear how to avoid it except through an extreme form of individualism, which is, of course, not all that communal.

Roman history, with its specific delineations between patrician and plebian class structures, fits the Marxist worldview more effectively than the individualist and competitive city-states of Greece. Nothing about Rome's history and culture is all that admirable except that Roman politics seemed to lack even an insincere veil regarding the desire for power. Tiberius Gracchus, who became a Roman tribune in 133 BCE, would be an exception to that generality as he wanted the wealth that the Romans hoisted from the Carthaginians to seep lower than the Roman political topsoil. Harman describes him:

> He was an aristocrat worried by the increased poverty of the mass of peasants and was motivated partly by concern for the military security of the republic. He could see that the peasant backbone of the Roman army was slowly being destroyed by the influx of slaves, while a formidable slave revolt in Sicily had highlighted the dangers in this way of organizing culture. (2018, 76)

Marxist historians need not torture their historical theses in order to describe Rome's problems. Class, genuine class (not the kind determined by consumer purchase), did disrupt Rome, first by revealing how corrupt the Senate was when they killed the Gracchus brother, but only a century later when the lower classes began to serve in the military and threw their support to Caesar was the revolution against the Senate really complete. This was after a "social war" (91–88 BCE) failed to fully reconstitute society.

Curiously, Harman fails to mention the Social War specifically, choosing to focus on the slave revolt led by Spartacus in 73 BCE. Perhaps this was because "Karl Marx described Spartacus as his favorite historical figure, and the German revolutionaries led by Rosa Luxemburg in 1919 called themselves the Spartakusbund" (2018, 79). Christianity, as a loose theology carried in loose-leafed gospels, appeared first in Rome. Christianity receives gentle treatment from Harman:

> The Christian message provided consolation for the poor. It provided a sense of their own worth to those of the better off who were despised for their humble origins. And it provided a way in which the minority of the rich who were revolted by the world around them could discharge their guilt while keeping their wealth. (2018, 95)

Was this a social function of Christianity? Charity, as a concept in itself, rarely receives criticism from anyone but Marxists. Charity ameliorates the condition of the proletariat and therefore only prolongs the inevitable revolt of the working class that leads to a Communist state. It may also allow for the upper classes to believe that the spreading of their wealth is a godly act. From this, one could easily conclude that the acquisition of wealth is a godly act as well. Christianity's appeal to the elite classes in Rome deserves more attention from historians, and this may be where a Marxist approach could prove to be the most useful.

Part 3 comes just a little over one hundred pages into the book, another indicator that Harman is simply more comfortable writing about the regions and epochs that Marx concerned himself with. After a short introduction, Harman writes about China and returns to the "people's history" theme:

> The plight of the mass of peasants went from bad to worse. In one region 90 percent of the peasants were reported to be "living from hand to mouth." There was a growth of banditry and "frequent rural riots, in which peasants participated." In the 870s a wave of rebellion broke out, threatening the whole empire. An insurgent army undertook a great march from north to south and back again to capture the imperial capital, Ch'ang-an, in 880. (2018, 108)

This raises another problem with transferring Zinn's "people's history" method from the United States to the world. Zinn wrote with the expectation that his audience would possess a basic concept of traditional US history and a good many would have picked up Zinn's book in expectation of reading an alternative to the "this president did this, and that president then did that" presentation of US history that was the norm in US public schools.

Harman cannot share this expectation; few English-speaking readers know much about Chinese history and are unlikely to be hungry for something that would upend a traditionalist understanding about it. A people's history of China, to take this one example, just is not nearly as subversive as a people's history of the United States.

For anyone who does know about China's history, Harman's treatment is lacking in seriousness. Why included a section titled "Leading the World" that includes "There was considerable technological innovation. Pit coal was substituted for charcoal in metallurgy, water-driven machinery was used for working bellows, and explosives were employed in the mines. The quantity of iron produced in 1078 exceeded 114,000 tons—it only reached 68,000 tons in England in 1788" (2018, 111). Why would he write this but not include a word about the notorious concubine turned empress named Wu (624–705) or mention anything about the breaking and binding of women's feet that began in the mid-ninth century? How can Harman not mention foot binding at all, and how can he have missed something that would have been so central to his thesis?

The answer to his question probably also answers why he would include only six pages for the Byzantine Empire and, even more egregiously, why he would title the chapter on the topic "Byzantium: The Living Fossil." The entire chapter serves only to degrade Byzantine culture. Two chapters in a row begin with "There were few advances in technology," and "There was not even a limited advance in science" (2018, 118). The passive sentence structure, lack of detail, and general dismissiveness of Byzantium as a historical force seem to indicate that Harman is including this section only to justify titling his work a "history of the world."

What does Harman make of Islam? Marxism stood in clear opposition to Christianity, but aspects of Islam, like the Ummah, do not seem antithetical to Communist ideals. Harman's treatment of early Islam reads much like the disinterested treatment he gave to China and Byzantium, but then there comes a subsection titled "Parasites and Paralysis," and the two paragraphs under it read:

> The Muslim Empire certainly provided a sharp contrast, not just to Dark Age Europe but also to stagnating Byzantium. Yet it suffered from gave faults which meant it never matched the dynamism, innovation and technical advance of China.
>
> First, the flourishing town life and culture was not matched by a corresponding advance in the techniques of production. The Abbasid revolution created space for the expansion of trade and enabled the urban middle classes to influence the functioning of the state. But real power remained with groups which were essentially parasitic on production carried out by others. The royal court increasingly adopted the traditional trappings of an oriental monarchy, with vast expenditures designed to feed the egos of its rulers and to impress their subjects. State officials expected to make enormous fortunes from bribes and by diverting state revenues into their own pockets. Even merchants who enriched themselves by trade would see speculation in land ownership or tax farming as more fruitful than investment in urban production. (2018, 131)

Can Islamic history be understood using a historical methodology, like Marxism, that developed outside of the Islamic world? Would US historians tolerate an Islamic take on the American Revolution that stated something like "The Constitution framers, without even a basic understanding of the Qu'ran or Sharia law, did the best they could to create a legal code for the newly created Untied States"?

Parasites and paralysis certainly beset medieval Islamic empires, but they were Islamic parasites and it was Islamic paralysis, that is, they were created from the conditions and ideals of the time and cannot really be understood using nineteenth-century Western class divisions. It might be possible to explain the social conditions of the Islamic empires though a Marxist framework, but it would require a great deal more in-depth analysis than is provided by Harman.

African history gets little better treatment, largely because little can be known and verified about Africa through traditional historical means, but here is the only place where the concept of geographic determinism, a major part of world historical studies since the 1970s, is mentioned. After explaining the basic "Eurasia runs east to west and Africa runs north to south, and east to west is better for the transmission of technology and ideas" thesis, Harman writes:

> Backward peoples in Europe—such as the British, the Germans, or the Scandinavians—could eventually, even in the Dark Ages, gain knowledge of technical innovations and agricultural improvements from China, India, or the Middle East. They could feed off advances made right across the world's greatest land mass. The civilizations of sub-Saharan Africa had to rely much more on their own resources. They were relatively isolated, in a continent half the size and with about one sixth the population of Eurasia. It was not an insuperable barrier to the development of society, as the record of successive civilization shows. But it placed them at a fatal disadvantage when eventually they were confronted by rapacious visitors from the formerly backward region of western Europe, which had been more easily able to borrow and develop technologies from the other end of Asia. (2018, 139)

This comes very close to the embarrassing and toxic vision of history offered up by the Nation of Islam. Both Harman and the nation tended to describe Africans and black people worldwide as a unified group opposed by light-skinned devils. It's a simplistic mythology not to be taken seriously, but Harman only adds a respectability to his thesis by incorporating geographic determinism.

Harman's reference to Africans, people who speak several hundred different dialects and who straddle three separate climatic zones, as "them" indicates a deep misunderstanding of ethnic and linguistic divisions. Furthermore, every historian of the European imperial era understands that the European empires themselves could not have functioned without the cooperation of the colonized peoples, who were usually divided and graded for the purpose of administering the empire. There never was a period of European imperialism, only a period in which

Europeans exploited and enlarged already existing gradations within traditional societies.

Only in chapter 6, "European Feudalism," does Harman seem to become more comfortable with his "world" history. He states this of medieval Europe:

> Europe's very backwardness encouraged people to adopt new ways of wresting a livelihood from elsewhere. Slowly, over many centuries, they began to apply techniques already known in China, India, Egypt, Mesopotamia and southern Spain. There was a corresponding slow but cumulative change in the social relations of society as a whole, just as there had been in Sung China or the Abbasid caliphate. But this time it happened without the enormous dead weight of an old imperial superstructure to smother continued advance. The very backwardness of Europe allowed it to leapfrog over the great empires. (2018, 141)

Did Harman read Alfred Crosby's classic *The Measure of Reality: Quantification and Western Society, 1250–1600* that was published in 1996? Crosby wrote:

> The West compared with contemporary Muslim, Indian, and Chinese civilizations, was uniquely prepared to survive and even to profit from such an avalanche of change. Western Europe had the characteristics that physicians seeking to counter the disorder of senescence hope to find in fetal tissue, that is to say, not so much vigor per se, though that is surely valuable in itself, as a lack of differentiation. Fetal tissue is so young that it retains the potentiality for becoming whatever kind of tissue is required. (1997, 53)

It is a general rule that the eloquence of the writing results from a mastery of, and passion for, the material. In these two passages, the reader can see the same idea expressed. In his work, Crosby effectively argued that Europe's lack of development meant that European society could develop into something entirely new and more dynamic than the settled empires of the East. His thesis is unencumbered by a theory of class division that seeks to be all explanatory. Harman needs to explain how feudal society in the West could be 1) composed of oppressor and oppressed classes and 2) prepared to "leapfrog" the more advanced societies of the East.

Virtually all modern world historians make some reference to how backward and/or unsophisticated Western Europeans were during the middle ages; it's become a coded way for expressing that the historian is not racist. If the white-skinned peoples were once backward and the dark-skinned peoples were once advanced, then race could not have featured in the development of a powerful Western society. As a practice, this is unnecessary and annoying and skews the narrative away from serious history.

Marx based his theories of class exploitation from European feudalism, and Harman seems more at home in this narration. By page 143 of a book with 620 pages of text between its covers, Harman has already begun writing passages such as:

> Like other ruling classes, the feudal lords were concerned above all with exploitation. They would use unpaid peasant labor to build a mill, force the peasants to grind their corn in it—and charge them for doing so. But for a certain period of history, their concern with increasing the level of exploitation also led some of them to encourage advances in the means of production. (2018, 143)

The ruling classes of feudal Europe simultaneously established the exploitation of the lower classes and developed improved means of production, all in the pursuit of profit. The profit motive drives both innovation and the exploitation. Harman concedes that religion shaped the medieval mind as much as the culture, which brings up the question as to whether Jan Hus of the fifteenth century and Martin Luther of the sixteenth century were proto-Marxists who expressed their class misgivings through religious protestations.

This is not an argument that Harman makes or even acknowledges beyond just stating the theological positions of Hus and Luther because he just mentions some of the names and dates as a way of providing context for the time period. He continues to be interested in class only; when writing about fifteenth-century Italy, he states, "The artisans of the towns could be more radical. Many were only a generation or two from serfdom themselves, and, like the surrounding peasantry, they faced starvation when the harvest failed. There are repeated examples of them clashing with the town oligarchies" (2018, 154).

Thus, the medieval working class existed before "The Birth of Market Feudalism" (a subheading). "For the moment," writes Harman, the free market "only occurred in a few gaps within the old system. But it was like an acid, eating into and changing the world around it" (2018, 157). The choice of "acid" as an analogy is simply not Marxist; capitalism does not corrode, according to Marxism, it creates: it creates innovation, exploitation, division, and, ultimately, the right conditions for a proletarian revolution. Harman should have been more careful in his choice of terminology because the Marxist cannot hate capitalism. To misunderstand capitalism is to misunderstand Marxism. Capitalism is to Marx what Pontius Pilate is to Christianity.

Part 4, "The Great Transformation," further reveals Harman's actual ignorance of world history as a subject. Leftist historians love to pillory Columbus, mostly because of the fairy tale depiction given of him in America's elementary schools, but Harman spends his time discrediting the already thoroughly discredited notion that Columbus discovered the world was round. Why not mention that Columbus was driven to the

West because the Ottomans controlled the more direct trade route, across the Mediterranean, to East Asia's consumer goods? This would fit into the thesis of a market economy driving both exploration and exploitation, but it would require a more thorough knowledge of the era. Instead Columbus and the Spanish conquistadors get the iconoclastic treatment so typical of late twentieth-century history.

Back on the continent of Europe, Protestant theology seemed to stir the German peasants into a general uprising in 1524:

> Luther was horrified by the rebellion. At first, like the urban oligarchies, he was critical of the lords for provoking discontent. But once the peasant armies began to make serious gains he threw in his lot 100 percent with the lords. He wrote a tract, "Against the Murdering Thieving Hordes of the Peasants," which urged the lords to take the most extreme forms of vengeance against the rebels: "They must be knocked to pieces, strangled and stabbed, covertly and overtly, by everyone who can, just as one might kill a mad dog." He wrote that the princes should "not stay your hand. . . . Exterminate, slay, let whoever has power use it." In a letter he insisted, "Better the death of all the peasants than of princes and magistrates." (2018, 188)

This paragraph might be designed to smear Luther with his own words and to show that Protestantism was too infected with religiously hierarchical notions of faith to actually cause social reform. Luther's words can be taken another way, though, as the mass of peasants might very well have looked like a massacring horde.

The medieval peasantry was essentially composed of illiterate adolescents, and Barbara Tuchman's 1978 book *A Distant Mirror: The Calamitous 14th Century* includes the fact that the lower sort would sometimes entertain themselves by nailing a cat, by its tail, to a tree and then headbutting the poor thing to death. The First Crusade included a peasant mass that was described by literates at the time in apocalyptic terms usually reserved for the Book of Revelation.

The Catholic Church certainly believed that the "people" or peasants could only be kept in check through the threat of eternal hellfire. The concept of eternal Hell today seems illogical and extreme, but the prevalent threat of hellfire might have evolved in an ideological arms race with peasant behavior; that is, the worse the peasants behaved the worse the afterlife punishment had to be made to appear.

People who could read, write, and reason were rare (and almost always ecclesiastical) in Europe's medieval period, and modern historians might at least consider the notion that these literates had good reason to fear a peasant uprising. The elites of the time period might be oppressors, but it does no harm to consider the totality of what those elites were oppressing. It's entirely possible that the frequent masses and rituals, reviled by post-Enlightenment thinkers, gave the peasants a schedule and routine that helped to keep their worst impulses in check.

Given this, Harman's treatment of the Thirty Years' War (1618–1648), which is essentially to throw up his hands—"Anyone reading about this war is bound to be confused by its kaleidoscopic character" (2018, 196)—and then state, "The only constant features seem to be the rampaging mercenary armies, the looted villages, the hungry peasants and burning towns" (2018, 196).

The Thirty Years' War certainly can seem befuddling; it was sort of about religion and sort of about political power (which describes the Protestant Reformation generally), but it could very well be seen as what happens when the traditional medieval authorities of the Catholic Church and the local princes in the region of Germany suddenly lost power. Peasants made up those mercenary armies, as pikes and gunpowder weapons, cheap compared to armor and horses, became the effective means of waging war. Maybe the Thirty Years' War gives credence to the worries that the elites had about a power to the people movement.

To be fair, Harman does try to give an account of the Thirty Years' War, but a simplistic Marxist thesis cannot be employed on a history this complex. The Marxist thesis may not be much use in explaining the Thirty Years' War, but it morphs into a hindrance when used to explain England's Civil Wars and the 1688 Glorious Revolution, which effectively forced the monarchy to cede the important bits of England's political power to the Parliament. Harman writes:

> Although the revolution was over, many of the changes survived. The monarchy's existence now depended on the will of the propertied classes expressed through parliament—as was shown in 1688 when they threw James II out in a "bloodless" revolution. The wealth of the propertied classes depended as never before on their success in coping with market forces. The large landowners increasingly embraced capitalist methods of agriculture. The growing portion of the population who lived in towns increasingly either employed others or worked for others. Guilds were no longer able to prevent innovation in productive techniques—by 1689 three quarters of English towns contained no guilds at all. Government policies were dictated by the desire to expand trade, not by the dynastic intrigues of the monarch. (2018, 218)

These political shifts are presented as less important than the development of a capitalist economic structure based around the concept of market competition: "Together, these changes represented something radically new in world history. The means by which people earned a living was now carried out in units which depended for survival upon the ability of those who ran them to keep costs below those of other units" (2018, 218).

One could view the years of 1687 and 1688 as being the birth of a new Western civilization established around three pillars: 1) science (Newton published the *Principia Mathematica* in 1687), 2) the creation of market-driven and expansionist (through European maritime trade) capitalism, and 3) the origins of a new type of republican democracy created largely through the force of the Protestant concepts of individual responsibility and congregational (bottom-up) control of the clergy. The Marxist must either dismiss concepts 1 and 3 as subordinate to the new market forces of capitalism or simply consider both science and democracy to be forces that continued with the exploitation of the masses.

All of this is to say that Marxism provides a limitation for world historical study and understanding, and one could even argue that Marxism cannot describe the historical and economic forces that it was actually derived from. The Marxist conceit just blinds Harman time and again. Take this section on the Enlightenment for example:

> The Enlightenment thinkers were not revolutionaries. They were dissident intellectuals who looked to members of the upper class for sponsorship. They placed their hopes not in the overthrow of society but in its reform, which would be achieved by winning the battle of ideas. Diderot saw no contradiction in visiting the Russian empress Catherine the Great. (2018, 243)

Of course, Diderot saw no contradiction in visiting Catherine because no contradiction existed. Catherine II should rank with Abraham Lincoln as the greatest political leader in world history. Anyone who studies Catherine's life will recognize her genius and humanity; no one suffered from state-sponsored torture in Russia during her reign. When a Cossack thug named Pugachev raised a rebellion in Russia's wild east in the year 1773, Catherine's loyal army defended their empress and her enlightened reign.

Can anyone doubt that Catherine, who instituted as much liberal reform as her position (a German woman who came to power when her boyfriend and his brother beat the rightful male ruler to death) allowed, was a better ruler for the people than an illiterate thug like Pugachev would have been? Diderot saw Catherine as an ideal ruler, as she was.

Adam Smith, and his 1776 publication *The Wealth of Nations*, is usually seen as Marx's antithesis. Smith certainly occupies Harman's attention and a central place the narrative of this people's history:

> Smith . . . argued against any attempts by the state to control trade or conquer other lands. Left to themselves, people would always exchange the goods produced by their own labor for a selection of the best and cheapest goods produced by other people's labor, he said. Everyone would concentrate on the tasks they were best at, seeking to perform them as efficiently as possible, and no one would have an interest in producing things not wanted by others. The market would coordinate people's activities in the best possible way.

Attempts by governments to favor their own producers could only lead to people expending more labor than was necessary. Such controls might benefit certain interest groups, but Smith insisted they would reduce the "national wealth." Free trade was the only rational way to proceed. (2018, 259)

Yet Smith, and Harman notes this, is not antithetical to Marx:

The logic of Smith's argument was to move beyond a critique of the unproductive hangovers from "feudalism," made from the point of view of the industrial capitalists, to a critique of the capitalists themselves—to see them as unproductive parasites, living off profits which come from the labor of workers. It was a logic transmitted, via the writings of Ricardo (who attacked landowners from the point of view of industrial capitalism), to the first socialist economists of the 1820s and 1830s to Karl Marx. The weapons which the greatest political economist of the Enlightenment used to fight the old order when then used to fight the new one. (2018, 261)

This is certainly not Harman's fault, but specialist historians created false classification categories that modern historians, for no good reason, tend to try to work with mostly just for the sake of common usage. The "Enlightenment" conceit obscures a greater understanding of an intellectual movement that might be better characterized as "post-Newtonian." If Newton could describe the nature of movement in the solar system through just a few basic principles, then the post-Newtonians sought to do something similar in 1) economics (Smith), 2) human populations (Thomas Malthus), 3) history (Hegel), 4) biology (Darwin), 5) geology (Lyell), and 6) history/economics (Marx). All of these thinkers, to a certain extent, sought to describe how complex systems find their own equilibrium if they are just left alone.

Harman explained that the Enlightenment thinkers were not radicals, but neither was Marx. He primarily concerned himself with creating an explanatory system with the notion of historical and economic exploitation at its core. All of this has led to part 6, "The World Turned Upside Down," which is where the French Revolution and its fairly obvious Marxist connotations enter into this people's history of the world. Part 6 connects the American Revolution with the French Revolution with the liberal and nationalistic revolutions that failed across Europe in 1848.

Marxism just cannot explain the American Revolution, and therefore neither can Harman. It should be noted that there has already been a *People's History of the American Revolution*, by Ray Raphael, published in 2001, that provided a fascinating look at how revolutionary mobs refused to respect their "betters" either in the courthouses or in the military. But the purpose of that book was narrow and within the framework of Zinn's original people's history; Harman is trying to make broad connections across time periods and regions.

Harman treats the American Revolution in historically responsible terms; there's nothing out of the ordinary in his statements about the traditional events that led up to the breaking away of the colonies from the British. The only genuinely Marxist interpretation comes at the end of the chapter with:

> the American Revolution was more than just a political break of the colonies from Britain. Out of the turmoil of the war emerged a society which had shaken off features which harkened back to a pre-capitalist past. The feudal rights of the great landowners in New York disappeared. The deference of people for the "great families" was shaken. Hundreds of thousands of people in the northern and central colonies were won to ideas of human equality and liberty from oppression which, they could see, should apply to black people as well as white. For the followers of the Enlightenment in Europe, the language of the Declaration of Independence seemed a living fulfillment of their ideals. (2018, 276)

This just simply is not world history. A better interpretation of events would respect facts and chronology. First, the Protestant Reformation developed a concept of individuality, congregational control, and a skepticism about divinely inspired rule. These beliefs inspired the English Civil Wars and the 1688 Glorious Revolution. The Enlightenment thinkers, post facto, justified the Glorious Revolution in terms of a social contract. The new English model became so popular that the American colonists were upset that they could not participate in it, hence the adaptation of the previously Irish cry of "no taxation without representation."

More broadly speaking, almost all of the colonies of the Americas became independent by 1825, and European colonial efforts then focused eastward on the societies of the "old world." These world historical explanations simply do not appear in the narrative as Harman just creates abbreviated sections of traditional histories with a Marxist slant. The world historical causes of the French Revolution might include: 1) the French monarchy went broke supporting the American Revolution and 2) the success of the American Revolution meant that two examples of quasi-democracies, one just across the Channel in Britain and the other a long boat ride across the Atlantic in the new United States, showed French reformers and radicals that government without aristocrats made for more than just good theoretical discussion in the coffeehouses.

Harman considers class, almost exclusively, as a factor:

> The complex interrelation between the monarchy and the various sections of the peasantry has led some "revisionist" historians to claim the revolution cannot be explained in class terms. The bourgeoisie, they say, was more likely to obtain its income from legal office, landownership or even feudal dues than it was from modern industry. Therefore, it could not have been a class standing for a new, capitalist way of producing in opposition to a nobility and monarchy based on feudal-

> ism. These historians argue that their case is confirmed by the small number of big industrialists involved on the revolutionary side and the considerable number of merchants who took the side of their king.
> Some of their factual claims are undoubtedly true. The bourgeoisie as a class certainly did not stand in unremitting revolutionary opposition to the old order. It had grown up within this order over hundreds of years and was tied to it, both ideologically and financially, in innumerable ways. . . . The mass of the bourgeoisie repeatedly hesitated in the face of measures needed to advance that model of society. But they certainly did not go into exile in disgust when it triumphed, as did much of the aristocracy. (2018, 288)

What exactly is the bourgeoisie, and when did the wealth from the new world wash away the old order and make these newly moneyed classes the new oppressors of Europe? One would think this would be a central preoccupation for a Marxist historian, but the narrative just never comes together into anything meaningful.

Even the Latin American revolutions after 1815, some of which genuinely were driven by the lower class, broke apart against the medieval feudal structure that had been transplanted there from Europe during the conquest and consolidation phase of Latin America's history. Harman writes:

> the victories were sour for those driven by the ideals of Bolivar and Hidalgo. They had embraced the value of the French Revolution and aimed not merely at getting rid of the crown, but at ending feudalism, freeing the slaves and establishing a full bourgeois republic. Hidalgo had even gone so far as to rouse peasants to revolt with talk of dividing the land, while Bolivar followed his victories by calling a "Continental Congress" in Panama to establish a "United States" of Latin America.
> The great landowners who dominated the continent were not interested. It had been their opposition to such radical talk that led to Bolivar's initial defeats and Hidalgo's execution. (2018, 314)

The underclass just never could take power, never could coalesce around radical ideas. The peasants and proletarians, in France and in Latin America, tended to balk when revolutionaries attacked Church privileges. Peasant seizure of land is not like proletarian seizure of the machines; the big farmers possessed knowledge and connections to the people of other markets that made it unclear how the peasants would use the land anyway.

Capitalism and market exploitation grew naturally and were described by Smith. Communism and egalitarianism were created as theory and then attempts were made to apply those theories to already existing systems. The contradiction of Harman's thesis is in trying to superimpose Marxist explanatory theories on a history that grew naturally without any of them; this is a variation of the same contradiction that Marxism/Communism contained as an actual concept of governance.

In 1848, continual discontent with the old order regimes again festered into revolution. Only Britain and Russia avoided the upsurges; Britain because liberal changes had been made and because the kind of patriotism that was needed to defeat Napoleon lingered on for decades, and Russia because the people who lived in the cold northern reaches were so quarantined from the science and democracy that they could not have conceived of a better way of life (with the exception of a handful of men in the officer corps, who did in fact revolt in December of 1825).

From 1848, the narrative jumps to the American Civil War, and this misses the key fact that Russians lost the Crimean War and that this, coupled with the death of the arch-conservative Nicholas I, led to the eventual freeing of the serfs in 1861 for economic/military necessity.

Again, Harman fails to employ the "events in parallel" technique of world historical studies in favor of just moving from one highlight topic to the next and providing a shortened narrative punctuated with occasional references to the impact of class. How could China's Taiping rebellion, or even the Prophet and Tecumseh's anti-settlement movement in the early nineteenth-century American Midwest (then the West), be left out of this "people's" narrative?

The only part of Asia that receives any analytical treatment is Japan, but after Commodore Perry bullied Japan, in 1853, into opening up to international trade, Harman writes this about Japan's forthcoming changes:

> This was a revolution from above. Its slogans were traditionalist and the condition of the mass of people was not improved one iota by the change. But those leading it understood that they had to go forward to capitalism if they were going to maintain anything of the past. They abolished the power of the rival feudal lords, making them dependent on the state for their privileges. They did away with the old distinctions of rank between samurai, peasants, merchants and artisans. The incomes samurai used to enjoy from exploitation of the peasantry now went straight to the state; any samurai who wanted more than a minimal livelihood had to look to employment with the state or private firms. Most importantly, the government embarked upon setting up new industries, under its control and subsidized out of taxation. When these were strong enough to stand on their own feet, it handed them over to merchant or banking families with close connections to the state. (2008, 367)

Why could Japan create a top-down and forward-looking model of reform and package it as a Meiji "Restoration" when Russia, the Ottomans, and China could not? This is the kind of question that world historians should ask and attempt to answer, but Harman does not. This inclusion of Japanese history only exists to create a world historical conceit before the narrative returns to the West and, predictably, the Paris Commune.

At this point, one might ask, "Has Communism ever properly been implemented, and if so, when and where?" Communist historians and sympathizers tend to point to only two brief incidents in which Communism took hold as a proper institution. The first time was in 1871, in France, right after the French lost the Franco-Prussian War. While the French army was out of town, Parisian workers created a new Commune that existed on behalf of the working people. This institution of Communist theory excited Marx, and Harman writes:

> Marx noted that, as the representative of the city's working people, the Commune set about implementing measures in their interests—banning night work in bakeries and the employers' imposition of fines on employees, handing over to associations of workers any workshops or factories shut down by their owners, proving pension for widows and free education for every child, and stopping the collection of debts incurred during the siege and eviction for non-payment of rent. The Commune also showed its internationalism by tearing down monuments to militarism and appointing a German worker as its minister of labor. (2018, 371)

The second time was, apparently, in Barcelona in 1936. In his memoir about fighting for the leftists in the Spanish Civil War, George Orwell famously commented on how the working class ran things there and that everyone expected to be treated with equality. Is that it? Is "true Communism" limited to a few months in Paris in 1871 and again in Barcelona in 1936? These are the two models of aspiration?

Part 7, "The Century of Hope and Horror," is primarily about the twentieth century, and, like other surveys of world history, this one makes too much of the so-called First and Second World Wars. Technology and capitalism, according to Harman, transformed Western civilization and chewed up human lives in the process:

> Capitalism had begun by taking people who were a product of a previous form of society and utilizing part of their lives—the part that involved slaving away for 12, 14, or 16 hours a day in a workshop or factory. But now it could profit from enveloping their whole lives—from the beds people slept in and the roofs which kept them dry, to the food they ate, the effort it took them to reach their workplaces and the diversions with allowed them to forget the world of labor. It became a total system. (2018, 381)

Here is an image of what Harman could have achieved with a more focused thesis and manageable topic: capitalism's ability to envelop people until they become total consumers, that is, people who define themselves only by their purchase choices. This is the source of a sociological shift in world history that may seal off the mindsets of precapitalist peoples from those of modern people in a way not fully understood. How did people *think* before there was "shopping"?

Harman is clearly more at home with this twentieth-century topic and admits that the upper classes drove certain types of reform, but always out of self-interest. "Concern with productivity," he writes, "also implied the need for education and literacy . . . the complex interacting processes of capitalist production now required a literate workforce (2018, 383).

Like Zinn before him, Harman tells of the labor forces and anti-war protestors, of the International Workers of the World (wobblies) who seemed to be on the right side of history but lacked the actual power of the ruling classes and found themselves settling for martyrdom. Unfortunately, like so many leftist historians, Harman discredits himself with his account of the 1917 Communist Revolution; he writes of the takeover of power like this:

> What happened was monumental. In 1792–1793 the working masses of Paris had pushed the most radical section of the middle class into power, only to see that power turned against themselves and its holders ousted by self seeking conservatives. In 1848 the children of those masses had forced a couple of their own representatives into the government in February, only to be butchered on the barricades in June. In 1871 they had gone further and briefly taken power—but only in one city and only for two months. Now a congress of workers, soldiers, and peasants had taken state power in a country of 160 million, stretching from the Pacific coast to the Baltic. World socialism did indeed seem on the agenda. (2018, 423)

The Soviets were not a "congress of workers, soldiers, and peasants," they were a conglomerate created out of the fear, hunger, and uncertainty that followed Russia's military collapse against Germany. A terrorist organization, the Bolsheviks, seized control of the events in St. Petersburg only because their terrorist-in-chief, V. I. Lenin, had spent most of his life thinking about nothing but an overthrow of the government; he was mentally prepared to take power at a time when a state of shock seemed to overtake the provisional government's political leaders.

Once Lenin and his associates took the Winter Palace, Lenin quickly ordered that several enemies of the state be lined up and shot, then ordered the same fate for the czar and his family. Historians who are sympathetic to the cause never seem to mention these facts; Harman does not either.

The years after the end of the Great War in 1919 filled socialists with hope. The old empires collapsed, and the ruling class had armed the proletariat under the pretense that the pressures of the military unit, the flag, and nationalism would keep those workers shooting in the right direction (that is, at other proletarians from other countries, rather than at the aristocrats who ordered the fighting). But the moment faded and the workers unions, globally, failed to seize genuine power. Harman writes:

> World revolution was not a fantasy in August 1920, with the Russian Red Army approaching Warsaw, the memory of the defeat of the "Kapp Putsch" in the mind of every German worker and the Italian factories on the verge of occupation.
>
> It did not happen, and historians of socialism have been discussing ever since why the Revolution in Russia was not repeated. (2018, 439)

Lamentations such as this reveal a fundamental truth of history that Harman and other socialist historians miss: civilization and hierarchy developed together and cannot be disentangled. Hunter-gatherer societies possessed an internal egalitarianism, but this was sacrificed when farming surpluses and technological innovation took hold in the Fertile Crescent and then radiated outward to encompass the rest of the world's people.

Humans may carry the desire for equality with them, as we carry dozens of other traits that evolved for life on an African savannah; the situation cannot be brought into balance. Socialist governments have usually been implemented when organized military/terrorist organizations seize power from above during a time when external crises upset the traditional power structures.

What of the colonies that were created by the imperial powers of Europe? Decolonization has always been a topic of interest for Marxist theorists. The Marxist psychologist Frantz Fanon, to take but one example, wrote two brilliant books in the 1960s titled *The Wretched of the Earth* and *Black Skin, White Masks*, both of which depicted the way in which colonization distorted the mental process of the colonizer and the colonized. In the case of Fanon, a Marxist perspective helped to develop an understanding of the underlying effects of oppression. Marxism, however, is less effective in describing the actual historical process that led to the "overthrow" of imperial regimes.

Of India's pre–World War II anti-imperial protests, Harman writes:

> The pent-up bitterness in India was expressed in a wave of agitation across the subcontinent in 1918–20. A textile strike in Bombay spread to involve 125,000 workers. There were food riots in Bombay, Madras, and Bengal, and violent protests by debtors against moneylenders in Calcutta. Mass demonstrations, strikes and rioting spread over many parts of India. A General Dyer ordered his troops to open fire on thousands of demonstrators in an enclosed square, the Jallianwala Bagh in Amritsar, killing 379 and wounding 1,200. The Massacre led to demonstrations, and to attacks on government buildings and telegraph lines. The first six months of 1920 saw more than 200 strikes, involving 1.5 million workers. (2018, 455)

When parsed out and analyzed, this paragraph makes less and less sense. Nothing in the strikes and protests led to a worker's consciousness and, while General Dyer gave the order to fire on Indian protestors, the hands that pulled the triggers were as brown as the hands of the victims;

a reminder that Indians colonized India as much as the British did. The 200 strikes and 1.5 million workers on strike seems less impressive given that a 1921 census indicated that almost 250 million Indians lived in British-controlled regions.

Indians themselves never could reach any kind of mass anti-colonial consciousness or mobilize effectively against British rule. The second fact here is especially embarrassing for left-leaning historians: the British did not "quit" India by choice; postwar circumstances, not Gandhi, forced the British to leave India. At that point, Indians, as a mass, fell back into their localized identities that were now expressed through religious nationalism.

How should a Marxist view the Soviet Union? Harman needs to answer this question in the final portion of his book and it's too difficult of a question for a single chapter. In order to frame the question effectively, consider a similar inquiry into US history: How should modern liberal democrats view the constitutional era?

The broad consensus is that the Constitution created the scaffold of a free and democratic republic, but that due to the circumstances of that time period, slavery and a lack of women's rights remained problems that could be corrected through the American Civil War and the political agitation of the women's rights movement. This is a clever historical line because it allows modern people to embrace the constitutional founders while at the same time recognizing the need for the development of a more perfect union.

The history of the Soviet Union does not offer such opportunities for this type of narrative construct. The Khrushchev line, that Stalin corrupted the pure ideology of socialism that Lenin ascribed, fails to withstand even a brief biographical analysis of Lenin. In fact, Lenin's "New Economic Policy," which allowed for the use of open markets in the immediate aftermath of World War I and the Red versus White Russian Civil War created the exact ideological outlet that Deng Xiaoping and the modern Chinese Communist Party have effectively exploited, that of single-party rule and top-down implication of capitalism as an economic system.

Modern Marxists can hardly embrace Stalin, but what to make of the fact that almost no one wanted to live in the Soviet Union? Why, in a worker's state, did workers' unions exist at all, and why did those unions cause so much trouble? Gorbachev would seem to be an example of a liberal-minded socialist, one who would have views much in alignment with modern Marxist historians, yet the implication of his policies collapsed everything. Harman does not answer the question of "how should a Marxist view the Soviet Union?" Instead, of the late 80s and early 90s, he writes:

> In September and October a wave of demonstrations swept East Germany, and its government conceded negotiations and began to demolish the Berlin Wall which cut it off from West Germany as a token of its sincerity. Later in November it was the turn of Husak in Czechoslovakia to fall, amid enormous street demonstrations and a one hour general strike. Bulgaria followed suit. An attempt by Romania's dictator to resist the wave of change by shooting down demonstrators led to a spontaneous uprising in the capital, Bucharest, and his execution by firing squad under the command of his own generals. In six months the political map of half of Europe had been redrawn. The only Stalinist regime left in Eastern Europe was Albania, and this collapse in 1991 after a general strike.
>
> No imperial power could avoid being scathed by such an upheaval in its empire. The national movements inside the USSR felt increasingly confident, and the divisions within the ruling group grew ever wider and its control over society ever more precarious. Gorbachev made a last attempt to take a hard line against the opposition currently, only to be thwarted in the spring of 1991 by a second great miner's strike and a huge demonstration in Moscow. (2018, 592)

Harman never tries to analyze how this occurred. If the Communist Revolution of 1917 was a genuine power to the people movement and moment, then how was that same empire brought down by protests and worker strikes just a few decades later? And this did not occur under the watch of some dictatorial monster, but under a perfectly and humane Mikhail Gorbachev, a man who was seeking to reform the USSR into something that would appeal to more liberal-minded socialists.

The demise of the Soviet Union makes no sense if one begins with the conceit, as Harman does, that the 1917 creation of that state was a genuine lower-class uprising that should have led to further disruptions of bourgeoisie states across the globe. If that was the case, then when did the Soviet state go in the wrong direction? It could not have been during Stalin's era, for it was under his rule that the Soviets defeated the Nazis in the Great Patriotic War, nor could it have been under Khrushchev or his successors, each of who either continued with preexisting Communist policies or who harkened back to Lenin for guidance. Only Gorbachev, who refused to use terror and military force to hold the Soviet state together, presided over the collapse.

The whole history of the Soviet Union only makes sense in relation to the longer arc of Russia's history, and it should be written like this: the Bolsheviks, and Lenin, existed as an underground terrorist organization, of which there were dozens or hundreds that existed in Russia. The Bolsheviks did not cause the downfall of the czar but happened to be there when events outside their control led to the czar's abdication. The provisional government that ruled Russia in the aftermath of the czar's abdication made poor decisions (including sending more men to die at the front), the worst of which was to arm the Soviets in the hope of fighting against a military coup.

The Bolsheviks seized power and, suddenly, the techniques they used as an underground criminal organization became the governing ideology of the newly formed Soviet state. This ideology allowed for them to defeat the Nazis, but it created a terrorist empire across Eastern Europe that collapsed when a new leader, Gorbachev, tried to reform it.

Harman ignores too much in his people's history. He ignores that nationalism in the United States allows for 320 million people to live relatively peaceably together, ignores that the deadliest idea of the twentieth century was Mao's backyard steel mill, and ignores the implicit danger that Communist bureaucratic bumbling coupled with nuclear science brought to the world through the Chernobyl meltdown in 1986. In his conclusion, "The Illusion of an Epoch," he mentions Fukuyama again, and after a lengthy explanation of Marxist ideology, writes this:

> The conquest of the world by capitalism has speeded up the historical process enormously. There was more change to the lives of the great majority of the world's population in the 20th century than in the whole preceding 5,000 years. Such sheer speed of change meant that again and again people were trying to cope with new situations using ideas that reflected recent experience of very different ones. They had decades to undergo a transformation in their ideas comparable to that which took the bourgeoisie in Europe 600 years. The fact that at the end of the century the process was not complete cannot be interpreted as proving it was not still underway. The history of the 20th century was the history of successive generations of people, ever larger in number, resisting the logic of subjection to the world of competitive capital accumulation. Once, in Russia, they were briefly successful. Sometimes—as in Germany in 1918–19, in France in 1936 or in Poland in the 1980's—they settled for half-success, only then to be defeated. Sometimes they were defeated terribly, as in German in January 1933, without even joining the battle. But none of this provides the slightest excuse for claiming the class struggle is over. (2018, 619)

The revolution is always near but never here.

Neil Faulkner's *A Radical History of the World* (2013) takes a similar approach to Harman's book, but will be briefly mentioned here only because Faulkner's book does not take as comprehensive an approach. As was mentioned in the introduction of this volume, *A Radical History of the World* is misnamed. Had it been titled *Radicalism in World History*, the book would be an important contribution to international studies—it's just not a world history.

Faulkner also authored *A People's History of the Russian Revolution* (2017), which puts him in the same publishing circles as Harman. Faulkner's *Radical History of the World*, originally published piece by piece on the web, is misnamed, but as a survey for radical movements in world history, it provides an important, and compulsively readable, account. An analysis of his book is not included here only because, as he writes in the introduction,

> A common criticism of the web version was that I had neglected certain places and periods; that the text suffered in particular from "Eurocentrism," and even "Anglo-centrism." This criticism was justified. I have done my best to correct it. There are, for example, fresh sections on Spanish and Latin American history. But I cannot claim that this is a truly "global history." (2017, x)

Faulkner's radical history begins with the same the world is going to hell conceit that Harman's does, but the writing is clearer and Faulkner simply operates with a more manageable thesis. He does not try to explain all of world history through a Marxist ideology; rather he traces the history of people's movements in different time places and regions. In this respect, his history is more similar to Zinn's original "people's history" approach than was Harman's.

Still, Faulkner is like Harman in that he misses the big things by focusing on class uprisings and those who rage against machines. Women are people too, and the upward movement of women from 1792 (with the publication of Mary Wollstonecraft's *A Vindication of the Rights of Woman*) should be at the center of any "people's history." Faulkner just does not see how the end of Chinese foot binding, the mobilization of female voters, the development of the birth control pill, and the arrival of the Oprah Winfrey show in the living rooms of Saudi women in the late twentieth century had a greater effect on global events than workers' strikes and Soviet revolutions.

The revolution may actually be happening, but it is unlikely to end in a workers' paradise. How about a worldwide femocracy instead?

FOUR
Francis Fukuyama's Political Theory of World History

As has been demonstrated in this book, modern writers of world history seem rather preoccupied with Francis Fukuyama's 1992 book *The End of History and the Last Man*. Fukuyama earned a PhD from Harvard and then entered into conservative policy-making circles. The rather mild thesis in *The End of History* was that history provided random experimentations in various cultural, political, and economic models. The collapse of the Soviet Union in 1991 meant that liberal democracies and free markets emerged from this process of experimentation as the most effective governmental model. History, as an experimental process, had indeed ended.

The End of History was a book of the moment, and the title provoked scholars and political scientists at a moment when the Soviet collapse created deep unease. Much of the foreign policy and scholarly analysis from the end of the Second World War up until 1991 focused on Soviet-American relations. The Cold War permeated American society, from the nightly news to popular culture, in a way that made it become part of the daily lives of Americans in a way that no other topic in world affairs ever had.

It might be too much to say that, after December 25, 1991, a good many American scholars, and just average Americans, missed the Soviet Union. This may explain why so many of the scholarly class (over)reacted to the September 11, 2001, attacks with so much excitement; the fall of the Twin Towers brought out a sense of the historical moment not felt since the fall of the Berlin Wall.

For all that, *The End of History and the Last Man* is a young man's book. Fukuyama was only forty when the book was published. The evidence he produces in defense of liberal democracy is impressive, but he continually references obscure seventeenth-century philosophers and especially feels the need to derive his theories from quotes by Nietzsche. It seemed a bit as if Fukuyama wrote with an eye toward his book one day becoming a Penguin Classic (which it probably will).

Calling *The End of History and the Last Man* a young man's book is not to insult it but only to say that the narrative was carried forward by the energy of youth, the power of that remarkable historical moment in the late 80s and early 90s, and a young scholar's affinity for the classics. Fukuyama's world history, consisting of *The Origins of Political Order: From Prehuman Times to the French Revolution* (2011), and *Political Order and Political Decay: From the Industrial Revolution to the Globalization of Democracy* (2014) represents a more mature approach to philosophy, political science, and world history.

The Origins of Political Order is introduced with an homage to Fukuyama's mentor, Samuel Huntington, who authored a book about the interconnection of political order and civilization that was published in 1968. Fukuyama's mention of Huntington is an important way for him to begin because, as has been mentioned, world history as a discipline has never fit well in the academy, where specialization dominates.

Academics who focus on broad explanations and world history are rare. Fukuyama's training suits his world historical project well though. World history suffers too much from nonacademics who often bring a lack of scholarly discipline to the discipline.

From the first paragraph of chapter 1, Fukuyama reiterates previous assertions about the primacy of democracy as a political system:

> During the forty-year period from 1970 to 2010, there was an enormous upsurge in the number of democracies around the world. In 1973, only 45 of the world's 151 countries were counted as "free" by Freedom House, a nongovernmental organization that produces quantitative measures of civil and political rights for countries around the world. That year, Spain, Portugal, and Greece were dictatorships; the Soviet Union and its Eastern European satellites looked like strong and cohesive societies; China was caught up in Mao Zedong's Cultural Revolution; Africa saw the consolidation of rule by a group of corrupt "presidents for life"; and most of Latin America had fallen under military dictatorship. The following generation saw momentous political change, with democracies and market-oriented economies spreading in virtually every part of the world except for the Arab Middle East. By the late 1990s, some 120 countries around the world—more than 60 percent of the world's independent states—had become electoral democracies. This transformation was Samuel Huntington's third wave of democratization; liberal democracy as the default form of government became part of the accepted political landscape at the beginning of the twenty-first century. (2011, 3)

It should be noted here that neither Harman nor Faulkner in their Marxist histories ever made any attempt to confront these facts about world history and democratic institutions. These facts regarding electoral democracy as a global norm should be seen, along with the global women's rights movement, as the two great historical trends of our time.

To put it simply and bluntly, in the same way that 1492–1600 is referred to as the Era of Exploration, or 1750–1900 as the Era of Industrialization, our current era (from 1970 to the present) will one day be called the "Era of Democratization and Feminization." Please try, if possible, to separate all negative connotations from the word "feminization" as in this context it simply means the development of equality among the genders.

Fukuyama's concern is with political configurations only and he seems a little exasperated with the notion that there is somehow a philosophical "answer" to the problem of the state. In a subsection titled "Fantasies of Statelessness," he writes:

> There is in fact a curious blindness to the importance of political institutions that has affected many people over the years, people who dream about a world in which we will somehow transcend politics. This particular fantasy is not the special province of either the Left or the Right; both have had their versions of it. The father of communism, Karl Marx, famously predicted the "withering away of the state" once the proletarian revolution had achieved power and abolished private property. (2011, 11)

Fukuyama's stance is refreshing but creates a problematic contradiction for a world historian. Political institutions, and therefore bureaucracy, might be essential for organizing human societies, but those institutions can calcify and prevent innovation. This was clearly the case in seventeenth-century "old world" societies like the Ottoman, Safavid, and Qing Empires. Surely, people living in those relatively settled societies, had they known about the chaos enveloping Western Europe, would have preferred to live lives of stability and peace. Yet the West's lack of centralized control, over time, removed any bureaucratic barriers to innovation.

The way around this contradiction is essentially to declare that liberal democracy itself emerged from the chaos of the West as a political institution that is respectful of the very chaos and innovation that created it. Liberal democracy allows for only a light "rule" of the people, and, to read into Fukuyama's thesis, liberal democracy is a universal system that just happened to develop in the West.

Fukuyama also criticizes the right-wing fantasy of pure free markets without government control or regulation but sensibly concludes, "It is quite legitimate to argue that modern governments have grown excessively large, and that they thereby limit economic growth and individual freedom. . . . But in the developed world, we take the existence of government so much for granted that we sometimes forget how important it is, and how difficult it was to create" (2011, 12). It is occasionally useful for anyone, not just historians, to appreciate how cities get planned, sewers get fixed, and children get picked up from bus stops. Ordinary governance is entirely reliant upon the sincerity of civil servants.

Good and good, but to make a political argument is not the same thing as creating an explanatory theory for all of world history. Fukuyama begins with a thesis that is narrow enough to be proved in just two volumes, but wide enough for a topic as significant in size as world history. This thesis also allows for Fukuyama to avoid the problem of early source materials and their "historical" veracity. By describing the creation of state institutions, he can avoid some of the problems inherent in trying to extract history (by the modern definition) from the spurious source material.

This process begins with human beings in a "State of Nature" (the title of chapter 2). Fukuyama understands a "state of nature" as a philosophical construct, something upon which Hobbes and Rousseau based their conceits about government. Government either kept selfish human impulses in check or robbed men of their natural born freedoms, according to Hobbes and Rousseau respectively. Before the arrival of anthropology as a branch of science, philosophers speculated about the natural state of man only for the purpose of making some statement about their contemporary societies.

Fukuyama specifically uses modern findings to refute the Hobbesian idea that humans are individualistic and selfish: "Everything that modern biology and anthropology tell us about the state of nature suggests the opposite: there was never a period in human evolution when human beings existed as isolated individuals; the primate precursors of the human species had already developed extensive social and indeed political, skills; and the human brains is hardwired with faculties that facilitate many forms of social cooperation" (2011, 30).

This may be true, but it's not clear if the philosophy of Hobbes can be refuted by a modern science that did not exist at the time that Hobbes wrote. Hobbes speculated based on what he saw in the seventeenth-century Western European society, and to scientifically refute his theory is similar to modern geneticists "refuting" the idea of race using DNA analysis. Race is a social construct, not a scientific theory, and a scientific refutation of the concept does not affect the social constructs around the idea of race.

From the Enlightenment philosophers, Fukuyama then turns to the modern scientists and delves in the evolutionary path of human beings. This provides another example of how world history blends various disciplines as it becomes impossible to make an explanation of hunter-gatherer societies without delving into anthropology. Most world historians tend to begin their narratives with the development of civilization as a way of avoiding biology, but that approach is inadequate given that the development of city life is so recent and that humanity's DNA evolved in hunter-gatherer bands. What is interesting about Fukuyama is that he chooses to incorporate religious belief systems in a scientific/anthropological schema:

> From a cognitive point of view, any given religious belief can be described as a type of mental model of reality, in which causality is attributed to invisible forces that exist in a metaphysical realm beyond the phenomenal world of everyday experience. This generates theories about how to manipulate the world: for example, a drought is caused by the anger of the gods; it can be appeased by spilling the blood of babies into the furrows of the earth. This then leads to ritual, the repetitive performance of acts linked to the supernatural order, by which human societies hope to gain agency over their environment. (2011, 38)

This is the appropriate way for modern scholars to analyze religion — as a byproduct of certain neurological impulses that evolved in an uncertain world. Modern historians should not feel compelled to treat religion as anything other than superstitions that calcified over time into cultural and political constructs that then enforced a certain social order. However, after the analysis of religion, Fukuyama finds a biological/neurological basis in not just religion but also the human desire to be recognized and to find a place within a hierarchy.

Neuroscientific findings contradict themselves too often for any broad political theory to be derived from them. Fukuyama simply never mentions the most important concept in biology and brain science: exaptation, or preadaptation. Exaptation should be a core part of world history because the human hunter-gatherer DNA has stayed the same as civilization has grown up around it. Human minds have to be pushed to find new uses in a new environment.

This is not a big problem for Fukuyama's thesis as he references biology only as partially supportive for this thesis, but world history as a field needs to clarify its relationship to biology and the other sciences.

Fukuyama excels when the narrative moves from hunter-gatherer societies to settled civilizations. The development of settled civilization meant the development of property rights, and Fukuyama gives a nuanced analysis of the difference between communal property, individual property, and kin-based property. This section on African concepts regarding land ownership is lengthy but provides an excellent example of Fukuyama's abilities:

> Tribal societies like the Nuer that are pastoral rather than agricultural operate by different rules. They do not bury their ancestor in tomb that they must perpetually protect, since they range over a very wide territory as they follow their herds. Their rights to a particular piece of land

are not exclusive, as in the case of land for Greek and Roman families, but rather ones of access. The fact that rights were not fully private did not, as in other customary arrangements, mean that pasture lands were inevitably overexploited. The Turkana and Masai of Kenya, and the Fulani pastoralists of West Africa, all developed systems whereby segments shared pasturage with each other while excluding outsiders.

The failure of Westerners to understand the nature of customary property rights and their embeddedness in kinship groups lies in some measure at the root of many of Africa's current dysfunctions. European colonial officials were convinced that economic development could not occur in absence of modern property rights, that is, rights that were individual, alienable, and formally specified through the legal system. Many were convinced that Africans, left to their own devices, did not know how to manage land efficiently or sustainable. They were also motivated by self-interest, either for the sake of natural resources, commercial agricultural interests, or on behalf of European settlers. They wanted to be able to acquire legal title to land and assumed that local chiefs "owned" the tribe's land, much like a feudal lord in Europe, and could convey it to them. In other cases, they set up the chief as their agent, not just for the purposes of acquiring the land but also as an arm of the colonial administrations. Traditional African leaders in tribal societies found their authority severely constrained by the checks and balances imposed by complex kinship systems. Mahmood Mamdani argues that the Europeans deliberately empowered a class of rapacious African Big Men, who could tyrannize their fellow tribesmen in a totally nontraditional way as a consequence of the Europeans' desire to create a system of modern property rights. They thus contributed to the growth of neopatrimonial government after independence. (2011, 69)

Nineteenth-century European colonizers created African "Big Men" as a way of developing a class of people who fit within the European legal framework. Something similar happened when colonizers instituted "hut" taxes or head taxes on Africans as a way of manufacturing a need for money. Africans who needed to pay a tax had to find employment with the only people who were offering cash payments for labor.

As Fukuyama points out, something similar had to happen in Western civilization for young men to begin assigning status for money making rather than for bravery in war. He quotes Tacitus on the Germanic warriors who, after having trained for and fought in war, considered farm work to be unglamorous. "Tacitus remarks," writes Fukuyama, "that in periods between wars, these youthful warriors spend their time in idleness, because engaging in civilian occupations would be demeaning to them. It was only with the rise of a bourgeois class in seventeenth- and eighteenth-century Europe that a warrior ethic was replaced by an ethic that placed gain and economic calculation above honor" (2011, 75).

One is tempted to see, in these comments, a presaging of the legions of modern man-boys who waste their days in a virtual reality, play acting at comradery and blasting away at pixelated beasts and bad guys. Surely these children wish, in some way, for a time when status could be assigned by holding a spear rather than holding a job.

Fukuyama sees Hobbes and his theory of the state as a Leviathan, as being largely positive. (This is a thesis shared by Steven Pinker as well.) Personal violence, slapping and punching, all sorts of physical trauma, and what might just be called bullying likely permeated all human societies prior to the arrival of the state. "We know," writes Fukuyama, "that virtually all human societies have engaged in violence, particularly at the tribal level. Hierarchy and the state could have emerged when one tribal segment conquered another one and took control of its territory. The requirements of maintaining political control over the conquered tribe led the conquerors to establish centralized repressive institutions, which evolved into an administrative bureaucracy of a primitive state" (2011, 85).

Governmental hierarchy originates as a form of coercive control over conquered people. This, according to Fukuyama, is the transference of hunter-gatherer egalitarianism into bureaucratic states. While there may be relatively little hierarchy within the tribe/family/clan, the act of subordinating and exploiting conquered peoples led to the development of exploitative government.

Fukuyama supports this idea with numerous examples, and what he says makes a lot more sense than the Marxist notion that history should be divided up into oppressors and oppressed as one's economic position can fluctuate through one's life in a way that ethnic or religious positions (as defined in the premodern era) typically do not.

Fukuyama's analysis only becomes shaky when the narrative turns to the early Islamic empires. In a subsection titled "The State as a Product of Charismatic Authority" he cites the sociologist Max Weber's (1864–1920) concept of charismatic authority, which is an authority based on the idea that a leader's power came from a god. Fukuyama then writes that "religious authority and military prowess go hand in hand. Religious authority allows a particular tribal leader to solve the large-scale collective action problem of uniting a group of autonomous tribes" (2011, 87). This is a dubious assertion, as plenty of conquests have occurred without religion acting as a military cohesive. It is true that Christianity and Islam spread initially only when connected to military expansion.

The problem, as is often the case with world historical narratives, comes when Fukuyama tries to apply his thesis about charismatic leadership to Muhammad. Fukuyama starts by stating, of charismatic leadership leading to military conquest, that "there is a concrete historical case of this process unfolding, which was the rise of the first Arab state under the Patriarchal and Umayyad caliphates" (2011, 87). What is concrete in this history?

As has been stated before, something united the Arabs and allowed for them to engage in rapid military conquest in the seventh century, but there's no good reason to think that the unification came because of a man named Mohammed. The fact that the Arabs conquered out of the Arabian Peninsula at precisely the moment when the Byzantine and Persian empires to the north started to collapse as result of decades of warfare indicates that the Arabs likely had probed north before but found themselves rebuffed by more powerful states.

Still, Fukuyama writes that for the Arabs, "Things changed dramatically . . . with the birth of the Prophet Muhammad in A.D. 570 in the Arabian town of Mecca. According to Muslim tradition, Muhammed received his first revelation from God in his fortieth year and began preaching to Meccan tribes" (2011, 87). The phrase "According to Muslim tradition" is maddening because the Muslim tradition was not created for another century and a half and could only have reflected the needs of the era upon which it was written, not an actual history.

Stating that the story of Mohammed is an Islamic tradition is not the problem; treating that story as historically verifiable and then using it as evidence behind a thesis is the equivalent of quoting a Bible verse to support a thesis in biology.

To point this out is to reveal a problem in the entirety of world historical studies, not to pillory Fukuyama. Yet he does go too far with "there is no clearer illustration of the importance of ideas to politics than the emergence of an Arab state under the Prophet Muhammad. The Arab tribes played an utterly marginal role in world history until that point; it was only Muhammad's charismatic authority that allowed them to unify and project their power throughout the Middle East" (2011, 88).

Not even Islamic tradition says this. The Muslims have always taught that Mohammed died in the year 632, and the four "rightly guided caliphs" who followed him were responsible for the conquest of the Middle East. In the same way that Augustus once presided over an empire in which the *Aeneid* was created, those caliphs presided over an empire that saw the invention of a Mohammed.

If there is one standard in modern world history, it is the comparison of regions where civilization formed with regions where it did not; such has been the influence of Alfred Crosby and Jared Diamond. Fukuyama cites the common reason—"The physical geography of Africa has . . . made the projection of power difficult" (2011, 91)—as to why large-scale empires never developed on the African continent. "There are relatively few regions," he writes, "in Africa that are clearly circumscribed by physical geography. This has made it extraordinarily difficult for territorial rulers to push their administration into the hinterland and to control populations" (2011, 91). This is simply true; no north-to-south empire ever developed in either Africa or the Americas, and both regions lacked both the horse and the kind of landscape that would make conquest on horseback possible.

But Fukuyama is a nimble thinker, not driven by a specific ideology, and he draws upon historical evidence as a way of supporting a variety of explanatory thesis. In some ways, his approach is similar to what physicists have done with M-Theory, which is to say that they (and Fukuyama) take all of the various explanatory models and just choose whichever one is most suitable to the situation at hand. When Fukuyama encounters China, he shifts his explanations in the same way that a geometer will have to switch from Euclidean lines to geodesic when changing from a flat plane to a curved surface:

> The chief driver of Chinese state formation was not the need to create grand irrigation projects, nor the rise of a charismatic religious leader, but unrelenting warfare. It was war and the requirements of war that led to the consolidation of a system of ten thousand political units into a single state in the space of eighteen hundred years, that motivated the creation of a class of permanent trained bureaucrats and administrators, and that justified the move away from kinship as the basis for political organization. As Charles Tilly said of Europe in a later period, for China, "war made the state, and the state made war." (2011, 94)

War is an enterprise, and housing, feeding, and moving troops, certainly requires a centralized state. In the case of China, "Bureaucratization began in the army with the expansion of service from aristocrats to commoners" (2011, 114). As is always the case, the desire to lend some type of philosophical basis to a military program of coercion and control eventually led the state to create Confucius, but this did not happen until the Han Dynasty.

That's not to say that a philosopher named Confucius did not live and teach during the Zhou Period. It's easier to argue for his actual existence than it is for either Mohammed or Jesus. Almost nothing is known about Confucius, or said to be known, except for the sayings that his students later wrote down. With Confucius, historians don't have to determine how much super they are willing to take with their natural. Somehow Confucianism did not morph into a "divine right" type of theory, one that would sanction any form of tyranny. Instead, Fukuyama writes:

> The Confucian idea that a ruler ought to rule in the interests of his people thus introduced a principle of accountability into the government of China. As noted, accountability was not formal or procedural but based rather on the emperor's moral sense as shaped by the bureaucracy.... These bureaucrats were custodians not of a public interest but of a hierarchical, kinship-based social system at whose pinnacle they stood. Nonetheless, there is something to be said for a governing ideology that asserts, at least in principle, that the ruler ought to be accountable to the ruled and that seeks to preserve existing social institutions against the power of the state. (2011, 134)

The Chinese political system rates four lengthy chapters (6, 7, 8, and 9), and this Eastern focus is not driven by any desire for Chinese inclusion in world historical studies but because China demands to be analyzed in any book about political power in world history. In some ways, Chinese history seems to be an easy fit for Fukuyama's thesis. India, with its messy provincialism and historically distorted sources, fits less well. Fukuyama titles his chapter on India (chapter 10) "The Indian Detour." India and China started out with similarly fragmented political structures, but, he writes:

> The two trajectories diverged, however, with respect to warfare. India never experienced a centuries-long period of continuous violence comparable to China's Spring and Autumn and Warring States periods. The reasons for this are unclear. It could be that the population densities in the Indus and Ganges river valleys were much lower than those in China, and less circumscribed, so that people subject to coercion could simply migrate rather than having to submit to a hierarchical social order. (2011, 151)

People tend not to like being subjects to the heavy taxation of a state made by a foreign power or homegrown tyrant. To sum up Fukuyama's idea, India had more hiding places than China did, and this may be why no empires developed there with the same social cohesion as the Han. Fukuyama notes that the other significant difference between China and India was in the social hierarchy of the caste system and that in China, the "religious" figures worked for the state and the rituals they performed were state sanctioned, whereas "in India, on the other hand, the Brahmins were a separate varna from the Kshatriyas and recognized as having a higher authority than the warriors" (2011, 153). Over time, he writes, this would lead to a rule of law that could hold even officials of the state accountable to it.

Writing came late to India, and it is hard to know much about the subcontinent's early history. Fukuyama writes that politics did not arrive until "the migration of the Indo-Aryan tribes out of an area in southern Russia between the Black and Caspian seas" (2011, 154). Those tribes split into different directions, heading to Greece and Rome, into Persia, and eventually down into India, where they conquered the indigenous peoples and established the socioreligious system of caste.

All of this is written about as a way of comparing India's history with China and as a way of stating that the two societies largely paralleled one another up to that point. A similar approach might be made with Japan and England up until the late sixteenth century, when both had similar histories and social structures, but then England "detoured" due to a series of historical factors. The India "detour" moment from China's history is explained as follows:

> The evolution of Indian politics diverged from the Chinese pattern in dramatic ways right around the time of the emergence of the first real states on the Indo-Gangetic Plain. The Indian states did not pass through a five-hundred-year period of continuous warfare on an increasing scale the way that early Chinese states had done during the Western Zhou dynasty.... No Chinese political entity during the Warring States period could afford not to copy its neighbors in developing modern state-level institution; Indian political entities did not feel anything like this pressure. The Mauryas by the third century B.C. were able to unite a large part of the subcontinent in a single empire, but there were parts of the region they never conquered, and they never fully consolidated their rule even over core areas. The empire lasted for only 136 years, and a political entity of its size was never again reconstituted under and indigenous regime until the birth of the Indian Republic in 1947. (2011, 160)

Here Fukuyama deftly employs a core world historical strategy, the comparison of regions "in parallel" for the purpose of drawing out similarities and differences. He then explains what accounted for those differences. India's developmental system, created less out of warfare and with a geography that allowed for subjugated peoples to escape, never developed into a centralized state like that of China, and this meant that the loosely developed caste system would serve as a watery hierarchy in the provinces.

Fukuyama focuses quite a lot on the Brahmins, India's bourgeoisie, and their role in the subcontinent's political and economic development. The Brahmins "limited political power ... by controlling literacy, a legacy that extends up to the present moment and consigns huge numbers of Indians to poverty and lack of opportunity" (2011, 171). This is why modern India, more than anywhere else in the world, contains vicious levels of poverty intertwined with cosmopolitanism and wealth. There were separate strains of social class that developed in the same region but with almost no real interaction or transference of wealth and few socially inspired laws to change the situation.

After a comparison of China and India, Fukuyama analyzes the character of the Ottoman Empire and its reliance on a particular kind of slavery, one that took non-Muslims and forced them into various kinds of service for the empire. Slavery manifested itself most significantly in Islam's military forces. Fukuyama describes the practice as follows:

> Throughout the Balkan provinces of the empire, a group of officials would spread out, looking for young boys between the ages of twelve and twenty. This was the *devshirme*, or levy of Christian youths. Like football scouts, these officials were expert at judging the physical and mental potential of young males, and each had a quota to fulfill that was set back in Istanbul, the Ottoman capital. When an official visited a village, the Christian priest was required to produce a list of all male

children baptized there, and those of the appropriate age would be brought before the officials for inspection. The most promising boys were forcibly taken from their parents and led off in groups of 100 to 150. (2011, 189)

The *devshirme* cannot be understood with a typical definition of "slavery" in mind. These boys were slaves in the sense that they had no choice in being conscripted into the military. Once in Istanbul, some of them received an elite military education to become officers and some became members of an elite *janissary* corps.

One might be skeptical about just how much status the janissaries held, however, as it does not seem to be the case that Islamic parents were eager to send their own children into service. Fukuyama also details that the Christian areas of Islamic rule were also harvested for their young women, who became sex slaves for the Ottoman elites.

Again, Fukuyama uses a key analytical tool that makes world history a special discipline. The question is, was the extensive use of slavery something driven by Islamic doctrine or was it the specific political and economic circumstances of that time and place that created a slave empire? Fukuyama makes no apologies for an Ottoman state that stole children and then forcibly conscripted and converted them. He writes, "No comparable institution ever developed outside of the Muslim world, which has led observers such as Daniel Pipes to argue that it was ultimately created for religious reasons specifically rooted in Islam" (2011, 191).

This certainly might be the case, especially if, as was likely, Islam was first created to give a mystical/religious backing to the imperial control exerted by seventh-century Arabic conquerors. The Ottomans, ruling centuries after the invention of Islam and Mohammed, created a religious justification for a politically expedient need. Fukuyama writes, "the Muslim system of military slavery evolved not out of any kind of religious imperative but as a solution to the problem of state building in the context of strongly tribal societies" (2011, 192).

As was the case with Harman, who either misunderstood or distorted the creation of Communist Russia and the Soviet Union and therefore later could not adequately explain the collapse of the USSR, Fukuyama's original misconception about the development of Islam causes him to misunderstand the *divsherme*. There was never a pristine "Islamic imperative" that was then used or ignored to make a slave empire; Islam was always invented for the purpose of state building and for upholding a male-dominated social structure. Islam was whatever the ruling elites needed and wanted it to be; no one was ever constrained by Islamic law except for the people who were supposed to be.

The interesting thing is that, in a later chapter about the role the Mamluks (Egyptian slave soldiers) had in the Islamic empires, Fukuyama includes a subsection titled "States as Organized Criminals" in which he details an academic argument that the "state" grew out of what amounted to an organized crime syndicate. Historians are comfortable stating such a hypothesis except for when it leads to a new understanding of the origins of religion. Fukuyama's eventual conclusion is that "the institution of military slavery that lay at the core of the Ottoman power represented a dead end with respect to global political development. . . . No one outside the Muslim world ever thought that it was legitimate to enslave and then elevate foreigners to high positions in government" (2011, 228).

Eventually, writes Fukuyama, the internal problems of the Ottoman Empire made full Westernization impossible, although attempts to do so did fend off a full-scale collapse until after World War I. These are debatable assertions, as are any assertions about why the Ottomans stagnated and fell. What Fukuyama seems to miss is the importance of that collapse, which might be the biggest geopolitical "event" of the late eighteenth and nineteenth centuries, given that the Russians believed they had a right to former Ottoman lands, that Greece and Serbia would emerge as independent, and that Wahabbism would form in the Islamic heartlands all as a result of the Turkish Empire's fall.

Still, Fukuyama's analysis is more than adequate, and with chapter 16 he turns to the West, where Christianity connected with the state and where the Christian religion would form the framework for the creation and destruction of political institutions. Fukuyama does make the case that Western politics was "exceptional" in the sense that it was the exception to the trends that occurred elsewhere. In Chinese and Islamic civilizations, state was never able to entirely displace traditional kin-based tribal and political units. The Christian West was different, and Fukuyama chooses to title chapter 16, about this difference, "Christianity Undermines the Family."

Frances Fukuyama is not a polemicist, and he must recognize that his argument could raise a minor scholarly ruckus, so he is very careful in this section to quote a number of academics. The inherent question to the topic is "when did the state supplant tribal affiliations in the Christian west?" Fukuyama writes:

> The most convincing explanation for the shift has been given by the social anthropologist Jack Goody, who pushes the date for the beginnings of the transition all the way back to the sixth century, and attributes responsibility to Christianity itself—or, more specifically, to the institutional interests of the Catholic church.
>
> Goody notes that the distinctive Western European marriage pattern began to branch off from the dominant Mediterranean pattern by the end of the Roman Empire. (2011, 236)

Marriage practices in Europe differed from those in the Islamic world or China:

> The Western European pattern was different . . . inheritance was bilateral; cross-cousin marriage was banned and exogamy promoted; and women had greater rights to property and participation in public events.
>
> This shift was driven by the Catholic church, which took a strong stand against four practices: marriages between close kin, marriages to the widows of dead relatives (the so-called levirate), the adoption of children, and divorce. . . . Later church edicts forbade concubinage, and promoted an indissoluble, monogamous lifetime marriage bond between men and women. (2011, 237)

Here is where Fukuyama's argument, as he channels Goody, elicits the kind of fascination that makes world historical study such a pleasure and necessity. After noting that actual scriptural teachings do not seem to be all that concerned with specific marriage practices, Fukuyama writes:

> The reason that the church took this stand, in Goody's view, had much more to do with the material interests of the church than with theology. Cross-cousin marriage (or any other form of marriage between close relatives), the levirate, concubinage, adoption, and divorce are all what he labels "strategies of heirship" whereby kinship groups are able to keep property under the group's control as it is passed down from one generation to another. (2011, 238)

Before parsing out the significance of this insight, it should be noted that there is, again, a misconception in Fukuyama's analysis regarding religion and power structures. To say that marriage laws had "more to do with the material interests of the church than with theology" is to misunderstand what the Church was and has always been.

Church theology was never all that influenced by scripture; after Constantine, the Catholic power structure claimed to be God's representative on Earth, which had the effect of meaning that whatever the Church declared on Earth would be sanctioned in heaven. This is a nifty bit of theology as it had the effect of putting the earthly institution in charge of celestial affairs. Given this, the Church's marriage declarations are completely aligned with the Church's mission, which was always to increase the power and wealth of itself.

Nonetheless, the eventual effect of the Catholic Church's involvement in marriage institutions was to enlarge its power into a legal arbiter outside of the secular institutions, creating a legal dynamic in the West that did not exist elsewhere in the world. Fukuyama quotes scholars who approach this historical dynamic from a property and law standpoint. It's curious that Fukuyama does not include the history of St. Anselm and Theodosius, given that this might be the specific moment in time when the Catholic Church established itself as a legal authority that stood outside of, and often superior to, secular legal institutions.

Chapter 17, "The Origins of the Rule of Law," begins with this assertion:

> European political development was exceptional insofar as European societies made an early exit from tribal-level organization, and did so without the benefit of top-down political power. Europe was exceptional also in that state formation was based less on the capacity of early state builders to deploy military power than on their ability to dispense justice. The growth of the power and legitimacy of European states came to be inseparable from the emergence of the rule of law. (2011, 245)

Fukuyama spends considerable academic energy defining the phrase "rule of law," and suddenly Fukuyama's conservative/libertarian background becomes apparent in his analysis. He quotes "the great Austrian economist Friedrich A. Hayek" (2011, 251) and his thesis that "social order was not . . . the result of top-down rational planning; rather, it occurred spontaneously through the interactions of hundreds or thousands of dispersed individuals who experimented with rules, kept the ones that worked, and rejected those that didn't" (2011, 252).

The question that comes from such an analysis would be "works for whom?" Hayek's thesis, states Fukuyama, is based on an analogy with evolutionary biology. Yet in evolution it's never clear which factor is driving the evolution: did "you" evolve to take advantage of gut bacteria, or did the gut bacteria evolve "you" to their advantage? In politics, no less than in biology, complex relationships involving symbiotic evolution and variations of exploitation evolve in messy environments.

From this thesis, Fukuyama stresses that European kings were less top-down rulers and "more like first among equals in a decentralized feudal order" (2011, 257). In that type of situation, the king had to make use of legal precedents and arguments in order to assert his authority over the various feudal lords. From this, eventually, came a chaos of lawyers who created a loose legal framework known as "the rule of law."

With this rule of law in existence, the Church's grew in power and resulted in the eventual conflict with the secular authorities, mostly over the issue of whether the pope or the king would get to appoint bishops. Fukuyama ask this question: "So why does it make sense to say that law based on religion created the foundations for modern rule of law?" (2011, 273) before answering it with:

> The existence of a separate religious authority accustomed rulers to the idea that they were not the ultimate source of the law. The assertion of Frederic Maitland that no English king ever believed that he was above the law could not be said of any Chinese emperor, who recognized no law other than those he himself made. In this respect Christian princes

were like Indian rajas and Kshatriyas, and Arab and Turkish sultans, who would agree that they were below the law. (2011, 273)

This notion of the Church as an arbiter of law that not just affected secular rulers but that seeped into family life and marriage made Christendom unique among the state powers of the time. It gave the Catholic church arbitration over matters that the king might technically control.

In China, Confucian bureaucrats and tutors might control the rulers, but their influence ultimately flowed through him and not through the power of their own institutions, a crucial difference between the development of those political systems. At this point, Fukuyama writes an interesting sentence: "The emergence of a rule of law is the second of three components of political development that together constitute modern politics" (2011, 275).

The European "exception" must be proved to be exceptional, and that means detailing how the religious institutions of China, India, and the Middle East developed differently. In chapter 19, "The State Becomes a Church," Fukuyama again asserts that Chinese law "was whatever the emperor decreed" (2011, 276).

India remained too messy to even make assertions about as the caste system provided a power structure but no bureaucracy, church, or creed beyond assertions of privilege. Even then, Fukuyama writes, "A Brahmin who presided over royal investitures might not be willing to consort with one who presided over funeral rites" (2011, 277).

All of this is recited in a brief summary as the author's real aim is to provide historical detail for the creation of Muslim political institutions. "Westerners," writes Fukuyama, "often think that the fusion of church and state is intrinsic to Islam while being foreign to Christian Europe" (2011, 278), but this constitutes a misconception. Fukuyama's point is that the early Islamic empires, in particular the Umayyad, look formidable on a map, but the power structure was loose and dominated by regional rulers.

Local governors exercised political control but generally housed religious clerics who made Islamic legal proclamations. This meant, of course, that the religious power structure would be just as fractured as the state power structure. In Europe, a centrally controlled church bureaucracy could hold sway over the mosaic of feudal rulers, but in Dar-al-Islam nothing like this occurred.

After making this point, the author returns to China and the Tang Dynasty, where much of the same political points about "Oriental Despotism" (the title of the chapter) are reiterated. This marks a problem with the Fukuyama approach to world history. He is essentially arranging the facts of world history around a thesis about political development. This will either mean that he must narrow his choice of facts to those that are relevant to his thesis or else continue to make the same points through a broad span of history. Because he is hoping to "explain it all," Fukuyama chose the latter approach, which means that his work includes a great degree of redundancy.

Through this process, a great number of modern scholars get thorough quotations and explanations. One of those scholars, Mancur Olson, believed that states arrived when mobile bandits became "Stationary Bandits" (the title of chapter 21). Stationary theft, according to Olson, comes in the form of taxation, which was usually pushed to the maximum point before it killed the host economy. "The only problem with Olson's theory," writes Fukuyama, "is that it isn't correct" (2011, 304).

One can understand why Fukuyama needs to rebut such a thesis since *The Origins of Political Order* has a positive take on political structures. The Ming Dynasty, writes Fukuyama, taxed Chinese farmers well below the maximal rate that Olson would have predicted. Such intricate internal arguments and refutations might remind readers of the great theological debates of the past, but such a process is necessary in Fukuyama's process of constructing his world political history. China's rulers were not "stationary bandits," but China nonetheless failed to develop a capitalist economy. Why? Fukuyama writes:

> What China did not have was the spirit of maximization that economists assume is a universal human trait. An enormous complacency pervaded Ming China in all walks of life. It was not just emperors who didn't feel it necessary to extract as much as they could in taxes; other forms of innovation and change simply didn't seem to be worth the effort. The eunuch admiral Zheng He sailed across the India Ocean and discovered new trade routes and civilizations. This didn't provoke curiosity, however, and the voyages were never followed up. The next emperor cut the navy's budget as an economizing move, and the Chinese Age of Discovery was over almost before it had begun. Similarly, during the Song Dynasty, an inventor named Su Sung invented the world's first mechanical clock, a huge, multistory mechanism powered by a waterwheel, but it was abandoned when Rurzhen conquered the Song capital of Kaifeng. The parts of the clock were scattered; knowledge of how to make it, and even of its existence, was lost within a few generations. (2011, 316)

The world historical question "Why Europe?" almost always corresponds with "Why not China?" Several potential answers present themselves regarding the latter question, but "an enormous complacency" is not usually one of them as historians tend not to cite cultural characteristics as major historical factors. It would have been interesting if Fukuyama would have explored the impact of the printing press on Europe and its nondevelopment in China as the press may have helped to create more than the Protestant Reformation and the Scientific Revolution; it may have been a factor in creating type A personalities.

Nothing drives the development of ego like seeing one's name in print. A well-written book achieves a type of immortality, and Chinese authors and inventors lacked the opportunity to write or be written about for a large audience. Modern social media has driven people to seek extremes in beauty, physical fitness, or weirdness, and the printing press may have had a similar effect on Europeans and therefore not on the Chinese.

Chapters 22 through 30 focus on Western political development in which Fukuyama states that European governments had to develop with the rule of law in mind. War pressured the creation of centralized states because, as he writes, "To engage in war, a state has to mobilize resources on a larger and larger scale. The need for resources drives higher levels of taxes and novel ways of extending the domain of the tax state to encompass more of the population and more of the society's resources" (2011, 332). To wage effective warfare in the era of science and industry meant political intrusion into the daily lives of people on a scale that the Catholic Church could not have equaled during its most powerful era.

This intrusion leads to a new narrative in politics. Fukuyama writes, "The story of political development from this point in European history is the story of the interaction between these centralizing states and the social groups resisting them" (2011, 332). This is a bold thesis, one better suited to a specific treatise on the development of Western history than it is to a book of world history (and dropped in at page 332 no less). To Fukuyama, the tension between centralizing states and resistance groups led to "accountable government."

At this point, world history reveals itself to be a field of study that's resistant to bold theses. To state a recurrent theme, world history is a big subject. Fukuyama intends to engage in a parallel analysis of "four European state-building outcomes and some of the reasons why these outcomes diverged from on another" (2011, 333). World history as a field should thrive through the study of "events in parallel" and an analysis of analogies between the groups, but the knowledge and skill needed to do this can challenge the academic skills of even the best scholars. Fukuyama identifies four types of states: 1) weak absolutism, 2) successful absolutism, 3) failed oligarchy, and 4) accountable government.

Given that Fukuyama is the author of *The End of History*, the reader can expect that volume 1 of Fukuyama's opus will end with reasons why option number 4 will emerge to carry world government into the future. In fact, "accountable government" is the third category that becomes the basis of modern politics.

The example of "successful absolutism" that Fukuyama chooses to include is a Russia in which "the Russian monarchy succeeded in co-opting both its nobility and gentry, and turning them into a service nobility completely dependent on the state" (2011, 334). Only under Ivan IV did this really occur, after his death and the Time of Troubles, and the

Russian nobility chose the Romanov family partially because of a familial connection to Ivan IV's wife but mostly because the Romanovs appeared to be relatively weak members of the boyar class. Tsar Michael, the first of the lineage, was a gangly teenager who was apparently too weak to hold the weight of the crown on his head.

From that point forward, the power of the tsar or empress rose and fell depending on individual circumstances and individual personalities. Fukuyama's assertion about the power of the state over the nobility and gentry holds true when studying Peter the Great, but the nobility could clearly block the reforming impulses of Catherine the Great just a few decades after Peter's death.

The specific case of Russia's background and history meant that the Russians remained isolated from the positive political transformation of Western Europe, but that had little or nothing to do with any continuing policy on behalf of Russia's tsars. Beyond the simplistic assertion that the tsar's decrees received divine sanction from the heavily bearded god of the Russian Orthodox Church, Russia's monarchs held very little in common.

Like Harman, Fukuyama holds the French Revolution up to be a central part of his thesis. In this case, France is the chief example for Fukuyama's first category of "weak absolutism." Unlike Harman, Fukuyama asserts that the economic condition of France primarily moved the nation toward collapse and terror. Fukuyama writes:

> When Louis XIV died in September 1715, his state was completely bankrupt. The royal debt amounted to almost two billion livres, not counting another six hundred million livres of short-term unfunded government paper. France's creditors had claims on future tax revenues stretching all the way up to 1721; debt service alone exceeded anticipated tax revenues for the foreseeable future. This parlous fiscal state was not something new, though Louis XIV's aggressive foreign policy had greatly added to its scale. For more than a century, French kings had been constructing their centralized state based on a set of unimaginably complex deals with local power holders, who traded various privileges and immunities in return for cash. The state had gradually encroached on the freedom of all its subjects, but only by mortgaging its own future to a legion of corrupt officeholders in an unsustainable way. (2011, 337)

The French nobility lacked "big picture" thinkers, and they lacked any philosophical framework for understanding how short-term problem solving could lead to problems in the long term. World histories, by necessity, tend not to linger too long on any specific epoch or region. For a thesis driven world history, like Fukuyama's, this method of world history can create issues related to evenness. Just a few years of French history receives more in-depth analysis than the entirety of the Ming

Dynasty. Thesis-driven world history may simply need to be defined as a different species than the "to explain it all" varieties.

One cause of the revolution, according to the author, was the failure of reformists in the 1770s and 1780s to alleviate the unfairness of a medieval French system. The French nobility as a whole seemed to think that the political structure of France served no purpose other than to allow them to lounge around in their powdered wigs and stockings.

In cases of deep unfairness, the most egregious example of that unfairness tends to become a focus. The tax rate of France, in which the clergy and nobility paid essentially nothing, drove the resentment of the masses in a way that it never quite did in Britain because "in England, it was the poor who enjoyed tax privileges. In France, it was the wealthy" (2011, 352).

The reason that the French Revolution itself rates an entire chapter is likely because Fukuyama knows that it presents a challenge to his thesis that the rule of law was a necessary and largely positive development. Neither England's Glorious Revolution of 1688 nor the American Revolution of 1776 are problematic for Fukuyama because the former was a power to the people moment driven by parliamentarians who wanted to check the monarch and the latter occurred because American colonists who liked the British system were not allowed to participate in it despite having to pay taxes to uphold it. But the French Revolution was different; the masses revolted against a state that had traditional rule of law values. The masses revolted against a medieval Western institution. Fukuyama concludes:

> The French case teaches a lesson about the role of the rule of law in political development. The rule of law that had emerged in the Middle Ages before modern states existed acted as a constraint on tyranny, but it also acted as a constraint on modern state building since it protected old social classes and customs that would have to be abolished for a truly modern society to exist. The lawful defense of liberty against centralizing monarchs in the early modern period meant defense of a traditional feudal order and highly entailed, feudal property rights that were incompatible with a modern capitalistic order. (2011, 353)

That last sentence about how feudal property rights were "incompatible" with capitalism can be explained with a nice analogy. If capitalism was the new economic software of Western civilization, then it could not be run on the old feudal hardware. When Fukuyama writes, "ancient regime was an early prototype of what is today called a rent-seeking society. In such a society, the elites spend all their time trying to capture public office in order to secure a rent for themselves—in the French case, a legal claim to a specific revenue stream that could be appropriated for private use" (2011, 353), he drops all the points he was trying to juggle.

A proper analysis of the French Revolution must simultaneously compare France to England, the newly created United States, and Russia. The English beheaded their king in 1649 and drove another one away (ironically enough to France) in 1688. This happened largely because the English embraced Protestant theology in the sixteenth century, while the Protestants remained a persecuted minority in Catholic-dominated France. The fairer English taxation rate that Fukuyama mentioned earlier resulted from this revolution.

When the American colonists broke from England, this was not initially because of any theoretical dissatisfaction with the English Parliament. The phrase "no taxation without representation" indicates that the colonists wanted to participate in a system that most of them were rather fond of; the English failed to give the American continentals the same rights that English islanders enjoyed, and this led eventually to the break. Thus, by 1789, both the British and the Americans had created systems that were more accountable to the people.

Yet this did not happen in Russia. So why did the Russians not revolt in the late eighteenth century in the same way that the French did? The short answer is: because of Catherine the Great. Catherine was no foppish dimwit like Louis XVI. When she faced a Cossack rebel in Pugachev, she initiated some meaningful top-down changes to the Russian political structure that genuinely helped people at the bottom of the structure. The French nobility could not conceive that a political system should do anything but enrich them as a class, and no real changes were made.

These factors were latent in French society until the crown's support of the American Revolution caused financial hardship for the nobles while at the same time providing ideological support for the radicals. Great Britain and Russia, having already made some forced political updates to the system, suffered not at all from the initial phases of the French Revolution. Even in 1848, it was every region of Europe but Great Britain and Russia that faced revolutions. Again, Fukuyama's use of these four broad categories is just a feature of thesis-driven world history; the approach brings problems of analysis with it.

Fukuyama simply has trouble using world history to prove his points, and he starts making his own definitions in order to make everything fit. Take the section from chapter 28 "Why Accountability? Why Absolutism?" in which Fukuyama describes why five separate political cases in Europe led to "four divergent outcomes" (2011, 422):

> A very simple model can explain this variance, which has to do with the balance of power among only four groups of political actors in the agrarian societies we have covered. These are the state itself, represented by the king; the upper nobility; the gentry; and what I call the Third Estate. This fourfold division oversimplifies things tremendously but is nonetheless helpful in understanding outcomes.

> The state emerged in Europe when certain noble houses achieved a first-mover advantage in becoming more powerful than the others — the Capetians in France, the Arpads in Hungary, the Rurik Dynasty in Russia, the Norman royal house after the conquest. Their rise was due to some complex combination of favorable geography, good leadership, organizational competence, and the ability to command legitimacy....
>
> The upper nobility might well be described as residual warlords who possessed their own land, armies of retainers, and resources. (2011, 423)

The writing goes on like this, with Fukuyama marching different groups in and out of his categories. When someone overexplains while at the same time declaring that the explanation is simple, this sometimes leads to a "this is not even wrong" theoretical effect. Anyone who has listened to a cosmologist labor through an explanation of string theory will have a handy analogy at the ready.

In fact, Fukuyama does have a lot in common with string theorists. His topic of world history is largely resistant to any explanatory thesis, and if Fukuyama has a single problem in his first volume it is this: he does not appreciate the effects of randomness in historical variation. Sometimes ideas arise in one region but not in others because someone in one region had an idea while no one in another region did.

Minute historical forces like individual personalities matter in history, and this throws off grand explanatory schemas. Fukuyama would have been better off making the case that accountability and the rule of law took a "drunkard's walk" (a term used by physicists to explain that particles are unpredictable and herky-jerky from point to point but nonetheless head in a specific direction) toward accountable government and that this eventually defined Western civilization.

Fukuyama's writing sometimes betrays this insecurity about his thesis. "Some readers," he writes, "may conclude that my account of political development is historically determinist. That is, by describing the complex and context-specific origins of institutions, I am arguing that compatible institutions can emerge in the present only under similar conditions, and that countries are locked into a single path of development by their unique historical pasts" (2011, 437).

No, Fukuyama cannot be accused of historical determinism by that definition; he makes no predictions about the future. What he missed is that the very factors of probability that make it impossible to predict the future will also defy any attempt to create an explanatory thesis for fully understanding the past.

The last two chapters of *The Origins of Political Order* restate the arguments made earlier in the book, another example of the overexplanation phenomenon that became more pronounced as Fukuyama went on. Ultimately, it is not entirely clear what Fukuyama intended to do with his first volume.

The first section compares European, Middle Eastern, Indian, and Chinese civilizations but then focuses on Western Europe as Fukuyama attempts to describe the development of the rule of law and accountable government through a comparative analysis of different regions. In order to create the comparisons, Fukuyama creates new definitions for classes of people, writes long explanations, recognizes his potential weaknesses, and then tells readers his thesis does not have those weaknesses.

To compare thesis-driven world history to string theory is not to be flippant. Theoretical physicists eventually gave up on a single "Theory of Everything" (or, if they haven't, they should) and just threw all of the discrete theories that explained not everything but something into a pile and called that pile M-Theory. World history may be headed to a similar place eventually, but before that discussion can be had, it is necessary to understand and analyze how Fukuyama's thesis-driven approach to world history applies to a more modern history.

Volume 2, titled *Political Order and Political Decay: From the Industrial Revolution to the Globalization of Democracy*, promises to fit the thesis-driven approach more effectively if only because Fukuyama's background as a political scientist more closely fits the material. One can imagine how difficult it might be to employ the methods of a modern political scientist to the study of ancient civilizations, and that tension between method and subject matter may have contributed to some of the insecurities displayed in the first book.

But big thinkers think big, and so Fukuyama will be forgiven for the overreach exhibited in volume 1, and volume 2 will be taken on its merits. Writers use volumes for two reasons: 1) because a work is too long for a single book or 2) to delineate a thesis and argument into separate pieces. When a work is divided into volumes, there is a recognition that while themes might be similar, a new thesis is necessary to be applied to new material.

Volume 2 was published in 2014, at a point when the repercussions of the 2011 Arab Spring had not developed into anything stable but when the hope existed that the Middle East might abandon historical precedent and become politically stable democracies. In the United States, the housing crisis reminded financial optimists that, even without a Soviet Union, capitalism remains infested with problems. Surprisingly, Fukuyama opens his second book by trying to consolidate these global events under an explanatory thesis. His book begins with:

> Consider a number of very different scenarios that have been playing out at the beginning of the second decade of the twenty-first century.
> In Libya, in 2013, a militia armed with a panoply of heavy weapons briefly kidnapped the country's prime minister, Ali Zeidan, demand-

ing that his government provide them with back pay. Another militia has shut down much of the country's oil production, which is virtually the only source of export earnings. Other militias were earlier responsible for the killing of U.S. ambassador Christopher Stevens in Benghazi, and for shooting dozens of demonstrators in the capital, Tripoli, who protested their continuing occupation of the city. (2015, 3)

From this point, he details the problems with authoritarian government in Africa, the aforementioned American financial crisis (the origins of which he tries to explain, in the introduction, by quoting scholars), Turkish protests generated by the increasingly authoritarian tendencies of Turkish president Erdogan, and the large-scale protests in Brazil against a government that wasted money hosting international sporting events rather than trying to alleviate the harsh conditions in the slums.

Of Turkey and Brazil, Fukuyama writes:

> What linked these protests to each other, and to the Arab Spring that occurred two years earlier, was the fact that they were driven primarily by the middle class. As a result of the economic development that had taken place over the preceding generation, a new middle class had emerged in both countries, whose expectations were much higher than those of their parents' generation. (2015, 6)

Such a bold statement of current events indicates that Fukuyama believes so much in the power of his thesis to explain history that he thinks it can be used to explain current events. The reason that historians don't typically do this, and the reason that political science has been removed as a legitimate degree option in many universities, is because politics defies any explanation.

As of 2019, the Turkish protests were checked by a "coup" organized by Erdogan in 2016 that allowed him to suspend civil liberties. In 2018, the Brazilians elected a homophobic right-winger in Jair Bolsonaro, and the Arab Spring undramatically collapsed into undemocratic political institutions.

After this misguided introduction (political theorists tend toward overexcitement when watching the news), Fukuyama's introduction calms down into a summary of his volume 1 thesis. The most important section of the introduction comes under the "Laying the Foundations" subheading: "The American Revolution institutionalized democracy and the principle of political equality. The French Revolution laid the basis for an impersonal modern state, much as the Qin unification done in China. Both fortified and expanded the rule of law in its two sister versions, the Common Law and the Civil Code" (2015, 18–19).

The Common Law and Civil Code will become the protagonists of volume 2, and through them the modern state with a rule of law and political accountability to the people will develop. Where does this all lead? To Denmark, apparently. In chapter 1 of his book, Fukuyama writes:

> In the first volume, I suggested that contemporary developing countries and the international community seeking to help them face the problem of "getting to Denmark." By this I mean less the actual country Denmark than an imagined society that is prosperous, democratic, secure, and well governed, and experiences low levels of corruption. "Denmark" would have all three sets of political institutions in perfect balance: a competent state, strong rule of law, and democratic accountability. The international community would like to turn Afghanistan, Somalia, Libya, and Haiti into idealized placed like "Denmark," but doesn't have the slightest idea of how to bring this about. As I argued earlier, part of the problem is that we don't understand how Denmark itself came to be Denmark and therefore don't comprehend the complexity and difficulty of political development. (2015, 25)

This paragraph requires careful analysis as it states a position that has been labeled as "neoconservative." The word "neoconservative" came to label George W. Bush and the foreign policy advisors in his palace after the 9/11 attacks. The neocons had it in their heads that terrorist attacks came about as a result of the dysfunctional political development of the Islamic world. Prior to 9/11, that dysfunction was a mild human rights concern, but after the attacks the dysfunction became an important matter of US national security.

In terms of US foreign policy, national security ranks rather higher than human rights concerns, so the neocons pushed an agenda to remake the entire Middle East into, to use Fukuyama's phrase, "Denmark." This was the ideology behind the 2003 US invasion of Iraq, and nothing more needs to be said about that.

Fukuyama's neoconservatism is a less aggressive species, and it needs to be understood as separate from the ideology that caused the Iraq disaster. The Western world's foreign policies should be designed to help the developing world become a Denmark.

This needs to be stated again and again because without a clear and positive foreign policy, the United States and the rest of the Western world tend to lapse into complacency driven vaguely by the question of "who are we to push our values on the rest of the world?" The answer to that is that "we" are the world's leaders of a functional system that respects human rights, and to deny that is to leave prepubescent girls in Afghanistan at the mercy of Sharia marriage laws.

This part of Fukuyama's paragraph is aligned with his "End of History" thesis from his 1992 book, but he rather overstates the claim about the importance of world history for his project. When he writes, "As I argued earlier, part of the problem is that we don't understand how Denmark itself came to be Denmark and therefore don't comprehend the complexity and difficulty of political development," he insinuates that an understanding of Western historical development would somehow help create a new foreign policy.

Does this mean that the West should try to support the development of a printing press and Islamic Protestant Reformation in Afghanistan? Should we try to get the North Koreans to send explorers across the Atlantic?

Clearly the historical development of Western political institutions is less important than stating that those systems work and should be replicated. Fukuyama spent considerable time in the first volume contrasting Western political development with India, China, and the Middle East. This is more valuable for his purposes because if one's goal is to open China to democratic institutions that are held accountable by the rule of law, then one needs to understand China's history and culture in order to begin that process.

There are always those who think that the United States should mind her own business and stay out of other country's affairs. There are also those who think that the Western models are simply not compatible with the history of other regions. Nothing in modern politics supports this view; our allies in Japan, South Korea, Taiwan, Hong Kong, and the Philippines seem rather happy with democratic and accountable government and would be rather put off by an exit of the US navy from the South China Sea. Even people in modern Vietnam, who have every reason to hold a deep animosity toward the United States, instead look to the United States as a check against the encroachment of China.

And to Fukuyama's point that international leaders want to remake the more dysfunctional areas of the world into "Denmarks," please contrast this with the nineteenth-century goals of European imperialists, who wanted to colonize and exploit underdeveloped regions, or of the twentieth-century Japanese, Nazi, and Soviet governmental leaders, each of who sought to impose some combination of enslavement, brutalization, or outright extermination on their neighbors.

Fukuyama has the right vision for the world, even if he overstates the importance of understanding world history in pursuit of that vision. A deeper analysis about the place of the United States in modern world politics will be written in the conclusion to this book.

It appears that the author intended for volume 2 to stand alone as it takes nearly fifty pages before he begins a new argument. That occurs in a subheading of chapter 2, "How the World Changed after 1800":

> The rate of economic growth accelerated dramatically around the year 1800 with the takeoff of the Industrial Revolution. Prior to that moment, which corresponds to the historical period covered in the first volume of this book, much of the world lived under the conditions described by the English writer Thomas Malthus, whose 1798 Essay on the Principle of Population painted a gloomy picture in which popula-

tion growth would outstrip economic resources in the long run. (2015, 43)

The point that follows this statement is that industrialization allowed for the development of resources that in turn could support a greater level of population sustainability. Fukuyama is too well read and too attracted to nuanced theories to put forth a simple "rise of the West" narrative from the point of the Industrial Revolution to the modern era. Instead he quotes Samuel Huntington's 1968 political science classic *Political Order in Changing Societies* and states Huntington's thesis: "[Huntington] argued that both poor traditional societies and fully modernized societies were stable, instability was characteristic of modernizing societies in which the different components of modernization failed to advance in a coordinate fashion" (2015, 48).

Fukuyama picks this apart because most "traditional" societies, in places like Africa, were studied only after colonization had wrought change. Instead of looking for instability in the middle of the modernization process, modern studies indicate that instability exists symbiotically with poverty.

Several scholars are quoted in support of this, and Fukuyama writes: "Almost all the authors systematically studying the phenomenon of conflict point to weak governments and poor institutions as a fundamental cause of both conflict and poverty. Many failing or fragile states are thus caught in a low-level trap whereby poor institutions fail to control violence, which produces poverty, which further weakens the ability of the government to govern" (2015, 49).

Yet having stated Huntington's thesis and the refutations to it, Fukuyama sees value in employing that thesis for understanding the Arab Spring of 2011. This is an impressive scholarly meta-analysis, and it is useful. However, to restate an earlier point, this analysis could have been made without volume 1. And this fact throws the two volumes together out of balance. Fukuyama the flag-waving political scientist and theorist is vastly more effective than Fukuyama the world historian.

In chapter 3, "Bureaucracy," the argument is that to study a government really is to study a bureaucracy and that, while "for many people around the world, the central problem of contemporary politics is how to constrain powerful, overweening or, indeed, tyrannical governments" (2015, 52), in other cases the problems that bureaucratic institutions bring can be almost as problematic.

The central piece of evidence for this argument comes in the form of modern India. There's no way to describe India, and traditional markers of economic development are not adequate for understanding the country. In the United States, indicators such as the gross domestic product actually do mean something; the gap between the rich and poor may be wide, but even the poor tend to have access to housing, clean running water, and food. This is not true in India, where, Fukuyama writes, "alongside the billionaire tycoons and high-tech industries, contemporary India is characterized by shocking levels of poverty and inequality, with certain parts of the country on a par with the worst places in sub-Saharan Africa" (2015, 53).

Sometimes these conditions fester over into revolutions when the poor become desperate enough in the worst regions. The interesting thing is that Fukuyama states that "India's problem is not an absence of the rule of law—indeed, many Indians would argue that the country has too much law. Its courts are clogged and slow, and plaintiffs often die before their cases come to trial" (2015, 53).

Democratic government and the rule of law both exist in India, but Fukuyama writes that the local government officials, with their disregard for competence and tendency to accept bribes, tend to exacerbate rather than alleviate India's problems. (Could it be that democratic institutions do not mean anything unless people have a sense of civic duty?) When bureaucracies work against the people, this sometimes creates calls for a strongman who can direct the government to at least some level of functionality.

While he acknowledges the problem with too much government, Fukuyama nonetheless reiterates the importance of public services and centralized governmental control. Modern states really cannot exist without centralized oversight, and this means bureaucracy. The author further argues that without the state there can be no redistribution of wealth. Redistribution of wealth, despite what the libertarian "taxes are theft" crowd thinks, keep society stable.

All of this was a roundabout way for Fukuyama to introduce the historical topic of Prussia, which was "one of the first European countries to acquire a modern state." He chooses Prussia as a case study because the Prussians "began to put together an effective bureaucracy before it industrialized and well before democratic accountability was introduced" (2015, 65).

Part of the reason that Fukuyama is so interested in Prussia is because Prussia's history differed so sharply from England's. Seventeenth-century England saw the creation of a modern democratic state (of a sort) in which Parliament put pressure on and took power from the sovereign. In Prussia, absolutist rulers dominated the aristocracy and, in the process, brought power together into an organized bureaucracy that carried out the orders of the sovereign. Part of the reason for this had to do with the vast differences in the level of competency between, say, Charles I and his brother James II and that of William I and Frederick the Great, both of who possessed leadership characteristics that Charles and James rather lacked.

Besides a tendency toward basic competency, the Prussian kings proved capable of centralizing the state, Fukuyama states, because they kept a standing army even during peacetime. The development of this military protected the Prussian kings and their government and forced a sense of participation in international affairs that could not be matched by other states on the continent. All of this moved Prussia, by the middle of the seventeenth century, to create a modern bureaucratic state.

War puts pressure on aristocracies and frequently forces them into meritocracies, but peacetime relaxes those pressures and allows for the upper classes to reassert their privilege by gobbling up military ranks and titles. This happened to Prussia (and would eventually leave them vulnerable against revolutionary-era France, which became so meritocratic that a young upstart like Napoleon was able to assert his military talents.)

Here is the crucial paragraph of the chapter, in which Fukuyama captures the precise moments of Prussia's evolution into Germany:

> In the years after Prussia led Germany to unification in 1871 under the leadership of Chancellor Otto von Bismarck the bureaucracy protected its autonomy from both the emperor and the incipient forces of democracy. The franchise was opened up to popular vote in gradual stages after the 1870s, and new parties like the Social Democrats came to be represented in the Reichstag. But the Constitution of the Empire protected the bureaucracy from interference with parliament; while bureaucrats could sit in parliament, parliament had no power over bureaucratic appointments. There emerged by this point what political scientist Martin-Shefter has labeled an "absolutist coalition" of conservative and upper-middle-class parties that supported the autonomy of the bureaucracy and protected in from attempts by new political parties to place their followers in positions of influence. (2015, 77)

The new German state allowed too much autonomy from the various branches of bureaucracy, and this prevented a full centralization. Fukuyama's analysis of Prussia-cum-Germany is impressive, but his emphasis on political science narrows his analysis purely to the creation of a centralized state and other important factors, such as the creation of the modern PhD system in eighteenth-century German (German in the sense of a pre-1871 region and post-1871 state) universities, are left out. The German university bureaucrats created the most important shift in higher education since Boethius developed the *Quadrivium* when they mandated the doctoral students provide new research as a means of receiving a terminal degree.

That may be the precise moment when education/science both merged and developed into an instrument of the military. This is ubiquitous in the modern world. Historians might one day wonder, for example, why someone like Harold Brown, who was a math prodigy and physics genius who spent much of his life in university leadership positions at CalTech and places like it, could end up as the Secretary of Defense under President Jimmy Carter, but that made perfect in the

1970s, just two centuries after Prussia merged scientific research with education and then merged those institutions with the military bureaucracy.

Fukuyama sees the subordination of bureaucracies to a central government that is accountable to the people as the goal of modernization. Prussia to Germany might seem like an odd example to use in this case because of the Nazi era, but Fukuyama concludes that "Germany, Japan, and a small number of other countries get high rankings for the quality of their governments and low levels of corruption in the present due to an inheritance from an authoritarian phase in their political development" (2015, 80). This is a smart argument; modernization occurs in a herky-jerky fashion, and the point is that when a state stabilizes into centrality and accountability, it tends to stay that way.

It should be pointed out that Fukuyama is not a linear thinker; he makes points about the past and then reiterates those points with quotes from scholars and examples from current events. More than any other world historical writer, he demands something besides endurance from his reader. So after having made the point about Prussia, he detours into a chapter and discussion on how corruption corrodes political institutions in nations with high poverty. This is an important chapter if for no other reason than it reminds affluent Western leaders of how relatively cleanly most everyday governmental functions get accomplished.

Still, the narrative link of the book runs from Prussia to corruption to the 2009 European Union financial crisis. In chapter 6, the reader gets treated to this sentence: "I will return to an analysis of the problems of democratic government in Europe in Part IV of this book, and the failures of institutions at both a national and an EU-wide level to deal with economic management" (2015, 94).

Such statements reveal another great challenge of world historical writing. How can the facts be categorized? The topic is so big that analyzing events can cause one to see connections across disciplines, and so a step-by-step/linear approach simply will not fit. If the author tries to take a historical point and make it applicable to the modern era, then he risks losing the narrative thread. For someone attempting a thesis-driven approach, as Fukuyama is, the alternative of plodding through one historical epoch after another really does not seem feasible.

At any rate, Fukuyama's point is that the Greek government became an anti-model in Europe for its incompetent bureaucracy. "The origins of clientelism in Greece," writes Fukuyama, "are not hard to find; it is the result of the early arrival of electoral democracy, before a modern state had an opportunity to coalesce" (2015, 105). Usually, clientele systems get pressured for reform by a middle class, but in Greece the bureaucracy somehow absorbs the pressure and survives. Cynicism pervades the entire system, and high rates of tax evasion prevent the government from acting as efficiently as it should. Government incompetence provides an excuse for people to not pay taxes, and the lack of tax income helps to create more incompetence.

Fukuyama continually compares Greece to the United States, with the United States coming across as the more favorable democratic institution. Curiously, the author does not compare the United States with the European Union, which would have been a more apt analogy given the size and population. The Greek debt crisis threatened the European Union because wealthy countries like Germany and Britain felt aggrieved at having to bail out the Greeks.

American financial commentators often noted that wealthy states in the United States frequently pay more in federal funds than they receive in federal services, and this creates conditions in which states like Massachusetts "bail out" states like Alabama and Mississippi every year. This is a nonissue in American politics, and one suspects that citizens in Massachusetts might even support such a use of their tax dollars. The European Union could neither enforce fiscal discipline on Greece nor inculcate a sense of European civic duty among the citizens of the continent. As an institution, it muddles on.

After Greece, Fukuyama employs his analytical skills to Italy, where provincialism and a low level of trust for the government created a relatively weak form of republicanism. The lack of strong state institutions means that a centralized government failed to take ownership of violence, and this allowed for the mafia to flourish in southern Italy and Sicily. Of the mafia's origins, Fukuyama writes:

> The Mafia—the first and sometimes only thing that outsiders associate with Sicily—is not an ancient institution that somehow succeeded in surviving into the present era. It, as well as the Camorra in Campania and the 'Ndrangheta in Calabria, had very specific origins in the Mezzorgiorno of the nineteenth century. One theory of the Mafia's origins is that the Mafiosi were originally gabelloti, richer tenants who exploited their role between landlords and poor peasants to extort rents from both. Diego Gambetta, however, presents an elegant economic theory of the Mafia's origins: Mafiosi are private entrepreneurs whose function is to provide protection of individual property rights in a society in which the state fails to perform this basic service. That is, if one party to a private transaction is cheated by the other, he would normally take his partner to court in a well-ordered rule-of-law society. But where the state is corrupt, unreliable, or perhaps altogether absent, one must turn instead to a private provider of protection and task him to threaten to break the legs of the other private party if he doesn't pay up. (2015, 114)

There are two real pleasures that Fukuyama offers his readers: 1) he generously credits other thinkers in his writing and takes great care not to present the ideas of others as his own and 2) he leaves his reader a little room to think. It is easy to see how a lesson about the Mafia developing in the absence of a proper state could be transferred to the existence of, say, the Taliban in Afghanistan. It's also easy to see how the example of the Mafia fits Fukuyama's thesis perfectly; where there is property there will be some kind of apparatus to regulate property rights and taxation. If a bureaucratic/political state does not do this, then a thug state will develop on its own.

The point of volume 2, to trace the history of modern democratic politics that is centralized and accountable, does not start to get proved until page 126, when chapter 8, "Patronage and Reform," brings up the topic of the United States and Great Britain in the mid-nineteenth century. The British and Americans, according to Fukuyama, made successes out of systems that the Greeks and Italians made messes out of. This was because the United States and Britain "both reformed their public sectors and laid the groundwork for a much more modern bureaucracy" (2015, 126).

The British swept away the aristocracy in favor of a class of "highly educated professional civil servants" (2015, 126), but the United States remained caught in the morass of a pay to politic system in which elected officials passed out offices to donors and people on the inside of either the Democratic or Republican machine, depending upon which side won. When political operatives in opposition parties are dependent upon the outcome of an election for their influence and livelihood, then democratic politics gets bogged down in campaign slime.

Four full chapters, 8 through 11, are devoted to describing the evolution of American politics and its evolution away from a patronage system. Fukuyama crafts an intimate and scholarly argument. However, a reader might wonder after reading about the development of the US Forest Service and being treated to this sentence, "It is impossible to talk about the Forest Service without reference to Gifford Pinchot's background and character" (2015, 182), if the author has not forgotten the scale of his project.

Chapters 8 through 11 are too intricate to be analyzed in depth because to do so would require following the argument so closely as to essentially rewrite and summarize it. But Fukuyama clearly sees the example of the United States as paramount to the development of modern "normal" politics, to the point of writing: "Other countries in the world—indeed, probably a majority of those in the developing world—are where the United States was in the early nineteenth century. They have adopted democratic elections and opened up the franchise under conditions of great state weakness" (2015, 183).

Provocative sentences like that are inserted throughout as Fukuyama moves so rapidly from a microscopic to telescopic view. Just a few paragraphs after his analysis of an obscure pioneer of the US Forest Service, he concludes his chapter with this conclusion:

> In building a modern state and overcoming clientelism, the United States had one big advantage over many contemporary developing countries: from the first days of the republic, it had a strong national identity that was rooted less in ethnicity or religion than in a set of political values centering around loyalty to its own democratic institutions. Americans in some sense worshipped their Constitution, which embodied universalistic values making the assimilation of new, culturally different immigrants relatively easy. As Seymour Martin Lipset used to point out, in the United States one could be accused of being "un-American" in a way that one could not be "un-German" or "un-Greek," since Americanism constituted a set of values that could be adopted voluntarily rather than an inherited ethnic characteristic. Successful state building is dependent, therefore, on the prior existence of a sense of national identity that serves as a focus of loyalty to the state itself, rather than to the social groups underlying it. (2015, 184)

With this, Fukuyama completes a lengthy analysis of how the American system of government developed into something unique: a system capable of overcoming the various "tribal" (for lack of a better phrase) identities that people inside the system might identify with. With this statement, Fukuyama has now described how it was that the United States managed to develop into a nation state that fits his three categories of a competent state, strong rule of law, and accountability. To use phrasing from his best-known book, this would be the beginning of the end of history.

If states that meet the author's three categories are the goal, then after a discussion of how such a state developed, it logically follows that there should be discussion about how to spread such a system. Chapter 12, "Nation Building" does this. Like a good scholar, Fukuyama begins by defining his terms:

> State building refers to the creation of tangible institutions—armies, police, bureaucracies, ministries, and the like. It is accomplished by hiring staff, training officials, giving them offices, providing them with budgets, and passing laws and directives. Nation building, by contrast, is the creation of a sense of national identity to which individuals will be loyal, an identity that will supersede their loyalty to tribes, villages, regions, or ethnic groups. Nation building in contrast to state building requires the creation of intangible things like national traditions, symbols, shared historical memories, and common cultural points of reference. National identities can be created by states through their policies on language, religion, and education. But they are just as often established from the bottom up by poets, philosophers, religious leaders, novelists, musicians, and other individuals with no direct access to political power. (2015, 185)

Is Fukuyama making a purely historical statement, or does he think that nationalism can still be created from the bottom up? Poets, philosophers, novelists, and musicians may once have helped to develop a national sense of identity through their works, but they have almost no influence at all in a world where human lungs are choked with smog, heat, and humidity and where the mind is polluted by whatever vulgarities flow through these vicious little rectangles that everyone carries.

There are "Four Routes to National Identity" (the title of a subsection) identified by the author, although "the first three of these processes often involve violence and coercion" (2015, 192). He has a realist's view of the situation at least. Those four routes include, in paraphrase, 1) Wrapping borders around peoples with already existing national identities, 2) killing off or exiling peoples who do not share the core group's ethnic or racial background (that is, "ethnic cleansing"), 3) assimilating peoples from different ethnic backgrounds into the language and customs of a core group, and 4), which deserves to be quoted in full:

> Adjusting posited national identities to fit political realities. All nation-building projects eventually run into practical obstacles to achieving correspondence between idea and reality, and it is often the idea that gives way first in the face of simple power politics. The identity question cannot be separated from the territorial question. Ideas can be adjusted in a variety of ways: territorial claims can be scaled back, identity can be shifted from ethnicity or religion to ideology or a more flexible concept of shared culture, or entirely new concepts of identity can be introduced to supersede existent ones. Changing the definition of national identity to fit reality is the least coercive and most promising path to national unity. (2015, 195)

Is this so vague a definition of a concept as to be meaningless? Not quite. Fukuyama probably means that nationalistic identity needs to mean whatever the people as a whole will let it mean at any given time. A national identity, even if weak, is probably better than no national identity. His definition, however watery, does embrace the idea that nationality is just an arbitrary way of arranging people, but the point of his books is that every other idea for arranging people is arbitrary too, so why not be governed by the arbitrary idea that works the best?

With these principles at the ready, Fukuyama devotes chapter 13 to analyzing what he simply refers to as "good government and bad government" as each exists in the modern world. By stating where government works and where it doesn't, the author presages the question of "why?" Why do democratic institutions thrive in certain parts of the world while withering in others? This is the guiding question for part 2, "Foreign Institutions."

Part 2 begins with an analysis of Nigeria, a country that suffers from poverty even while practically floating on oil. Nigeria's poverty and low standard of life result from a political system that runs on bribes and violence. Fukuyama tells a story of how politicians and the police bullied a German soybean farmer named Robert right out of the country as they tried to coerce him into paying bribes. The result of this being "once Robert left the country, there was no one from whom they [police and politicians] could extract a bribe, no one further to tax. The potential win-win became a lose-lose" (2015, 218). To be bad at government is one thing, but to be bad at bad government is another entirely.

Colonial history, Western exploitation, US foreign policy, etc. cannot be blamed for Nigeria's problems. The country's oil wealth is controlled by black, not white, hands, but those at the top of the Nigerian political system refuse to share the profits widely, and there is no accountable government to force them to. Truly outlandish population growth threatens any sense of progressive reform. Nigeria is roughly the same size as Texas and Colorado put together, but those states have about 35 million people between them. Nigeria currently has 200 million people. So, imagine pushing those states together and adding 165 million people while subtracting most of the clean running water and just about all of the birth control, and you can get a sense of the challenges that still exist for the developing world.

Nigeria's recent history as a dictatorship turned democracy makes it an especially interesting case study and therefore a potential challenge to Fukuyama's thesis. A 1966 military coup led to a civil war, at least a million (and maybe many more) deaths, and finally the 1999 establishment of a weak republic. Of this, the author writes:

> The presence or absence of formal democracy has made very little difference either to Nigeria's rate of economic growth or to the quality of government. The performance of the economy is linked almost exclusively to global commodity prices, given the country's heavy energy-export dependence. Thus the country's economy grew under military rulers in the 1970's, shrank under both civilian and military rulers during the oil price collapse of the 1980's and early 1990's, and then rose again in the 2000s under civilian governments as prices increased. Neither poverty rates, health outcomes, levels of corruption, nor income distribution have shown much correlation to the type of regime. (2015, 223)

To explain, Fukuyama puts forth the thesis of an academic named Richard Joseph who claims that massive oil reserves have empowered Nigeria's elite to make fortunes but given them no incentive to redistribute wealth or to make contributions to the country as a whole. These elites face no accountability because, Fukuyama writes, "all poor people—the 70 percent of the population below the poverty line—in theory have a common interest in ending corruption and redistributing those resources more fairly, they are divided into more than 250 ethnic and religious communities that do not want to work with one another" (2015, 224).

The difficulty involved in imposing nationalism, and a particular kind of nationalism, on people who define themselves through traditional groupings is *the* problem that needs to be overcome in nearly every part of the developing world. A sense of public ethics and civic engagement follows from a nationalist sentiment. American readers might roll their eyes at such a statement when considering the American Congress and other federal institutions, but that's not really the best example of democracy and accountability.

Fukuyama never quite gets around to saying this, but American democracy works because mayors and city councils want to help people. Police officers do not, by and large, pull people over and ask for bribes, and elementary teachers genuinely want children to learn how to read and complete basic mathematical computations. All of this is built, in a way, upon a sense of nationalism. Nigeria, overwhelmed by population growth, is unlikely to develop the kinds of governmental institutions that are necessary to alleviate all of the other problems the country faces.

Other factors in determining the success or failure of nations involve geography and natural resources. This is a bland statement for a basic world historical notion, but Fukuyama writes two lengthy chapters on how a country's geographic conditions tend to influence the development of their political systems. There is nothing wrong with his analysis, but in a thesis-driven history, the author has to keep making the same points over and over, and this makes for tedious reading when the content is so well known.

Throughout those chapters, Fukuyama continues to give due credit to the best scholars working in that field, but one does not read Fukuyama for a historical summation of the factors that led to the development of governance; readers want to know what Fukuyama makes of modern China. The economic success of China since the 1970s has made the country a superpower again, and no major democratic political reform has occurred there or appears to be in the process. After detailing the different trajectories that Britain and China took in the nineteenth century and all the problems this caused China, Fukuyama begins his process of analyzing why China is different:

> China represents the one world civilization that never developed a true rule of law. In ancient Israel, the Christian West, the Muslim world, and India, law originated in a transcendental religion and was interpreted and implemented by a hierarchy of religious scholars and jurists. The keepers of the law in each case were a social groups separate from the political authorities—Jewish judges, Hindu Brahmins, Catholic priests and bishops, the Muslim ulama. The degree to which law limited the arbitrary power of rulers depended on the institutional separation of the legal-religious hierarchy from the political one, as well as the degree to which one or the other group was united or divided. This separation was the most dramatic in Western Europe, where the inves-

titure conflict of the late eleventh century resulted in the Catholic church's ability to appoint its own priests and bishops. In stark contrast to China, the rule of law was established well before the creation of modern states, and law put limits on state building that did not exist in China. (2015, 357)

This makes the concept of "accountable government" more alien to China than to any other large nation. Before it is possible understand the 1978 Chinese economic reforms that have created the modern Chinese system, it is necessary to understand the humiliations forced on China by foreign powers in the nineteenth and early to mid-twentieth century, followed by the trauma wrought on the Chinese people by Mao.

"It is impossible to understand," writes Fukuyama, "the China that emerged after the death of Mao and the reforms that began in 1978 except in relation to the trauma experienced by those who lived through the Cultural Revolution" (2015, 362). This is because Mao's eventual successor, Deng Xiaoping, entered his office with the belief that nothing like Mao or the Cultural Revolution could be inflicted upon the Chinese people again.

China's post-1978 reforms, led originally by Deng, amounted to new Chinese Communist party visions rather than any structural change to China's politics. Fukuyama describes the difference between China and the West:

> While contemporary China is increasingly rule governed, it does not possess Western-style property rights and contract enforcement. Theoretically, the government has not conceded the principle of private ownership, nor has it created a legal system that takes on the fundamental duty to protect private property. Chinese law, courts, litigation, arbitration, and a host of legal or quasi-legal undertakings have mushroomed in the three decades since the beginning of the reform period. But the judiciary still does not have anything like the stature and independence that courts do in Europe, North America, and Japan. Western businesses operating in China face a complicated terrain. While there have been increasingly clear rules promulgated regarding foreign investment, for example, many foreigners find that their Chinese partners treat the contract less as an enforceable legal document than as a symbol of a personal relationship between them. Particularly when dealing with powerful and politically well-connected entities like the state-owned enterprises, they have found that their rights are not protected. (2015, 367)

By seeking to compare China's property rights and business culture with their parallels in the West, Fukuyama misses something about China's internal Communist ideology. After 1492, all reform efforts in Old World society required an insincere veneer that made it look like the reform was a return to a traditional past. Even the nineteenth-century Tanzimat Reforms in the Ottoman Empire and the 1868 "Meiji Restoration" in Japan were couched as back to the past reform efforts rather than modernization movements. The fact that the most rapid and effective industrialization to empire process, that of Japan's, was referred to as a "restoration" showcases the need for the people in Old World societies to identify with tradition.

Thus, when the Chinese Communist Party sought to modernize their economy, they could not do so without some ideological cover. Deng justified a program in which a single-party state manipulates top-down market reforms by dusting off V. I. Lenin's "New Economic Policy" or NEP. Lenin implemented open markets for farmers as a practical way of alleviating famine in the aftermath of the red versus white civil war. The NEP was not a reform movement but a strategic retreat from the Communist Party's goals.

With the NEP as the basis, the Chinese Communist Party is certainly not seeking to implement Western legal rules involving property ownership and individual contract law; instead the Chinese Communist Party rules with a light touch in order to prevent revolution. Chinese people can buy and sell all they want, goes the thinking, but all of this can and does occur without empowering individuals as property-owning agents who have a right to hold the government accountable.

Despite this critical omission, Fukuyama rightly concludes that there is no positive evolution in China toward a rule of law. Instead Xi Jinping, the current "president," continues to centralize power and is increasingly becoming a synthesis of a CEO and an emperor. If history has not ended, it is not because of random acts of Islamic terror but because of the clearly planned direction of the Chinese Communist Party.

Following chapter 24, "The Struggle for Law in China," is chapter 25, "The Reinvention of the Chinese State." Fukuyama makes this statement regarding China:

> I would argue that the state that has emerged in China since the beginning of the reforms in 1978 bears more resemblance to [Han] classical Chinese state than it does to the Maoist state that preceded it, or even to the Soviet state that China tried to copy. Contemporary China has been engaged in the recovery of a long-standing historical tradition, whether or not participants in that process were aware of what they were doing. (2015, 371)

This is flawed analysis, and it collapses Fukuyama's entire understanding of the current Chinese Communists, which must be understood in terms of their Marxist and Maoist ideological origins. Communist China is like the Soviet Union but with four crucial differences. Because Fukuyama missed these differences, he sees China as being more like the Han Dynasty in its centralized political structure than like the USSR. The four differences are as follows:

1. The Chinese people traditionally hold little affection for Western culture or religion. Christian missionaries wrought havoc on China's internal social structure in the nineteenth century, precipitating the Taiping Dynasty, and even before that, the British insistence on privileged legal status for missionaries alienated most Chinese people. China will have no equivalent of Poland, where an actual Church bureaucracy opposed the Soviet government in Moscow. Furthermore, in the 1960s, when "Beatlemania" infected the young people of Russia, the opposite occurred in China. Young people rejected Western music and culture, and instead hyperventilated over Mao. The factors that corroded the Soviet state are not inherent in China.
2. The Chinese will never have a Gorbachev. American policy analysts give the American-led "arms race" too much credit in collapsing the Soviet Union. Both the Pakistanis and the Chinese forced serious deprivations on their people in the twentieth century without collapsing. By trying to reform the Soviet model, Gorbachev facilitated its destruction (he could not have done more to destroy the Soviet Union if he had been a CIA plant). No one like Gorbachev will ever be the head of the Chinese Communist Party.
3. The traditional political science theory regarding state power and capitalism has it that capitalism creates a middle class that then pressures the government for economic reform. If a state is successful in creating top-down capitalism, then it will create the class that destroys the state. How is the Chinese Communist Party simultaneously creating a middle class and preventing democratic political reform?

    The answer is that they are not doing this. Instead the Chinese government outsources tens of millions of educated engineers and entrepreneurs into Africa and Pakistan; the former is occurring at such a scale that the journalist Howard W. French calls Africa "China's Second Continent" (the title of his excellent book). In addition, the one child policy and the skewed male to female ratio in China prevented the creation of a large middle "class" of young families who might advocate for a greater level of political participation. Men who are looking for women are not looking for political reform. In addition, much of China's GDP growth is connected to "make work" policies like the construction of houses, buildings, and even cities where no one lives.
4. The Communist Party in China, since 1978, has largely behaved with internal competency and external restraint. The Chinese can be aggressive toward neighbors that they consider to be in Chinese territory, but rounding up Muslims in the West is ethically repulsive, it is not politically disastrous. The Chinese will not invade Afghanistan as the Soviets did, nor will Chinese scientists preside

over the collapse of a nuclear reactor as was the case in Chernobyl. China's Communist Party can be both corrupt and Mafia like, but they usually only deal with problems in their own family.

Because Fukuyama misses these four points, he can see China only through the prism of political analysis that he has constructed. Instead of recognizing that China has outsourced much of its middle class or coopted them to the cause as a result an educational system that focuses on the humiliations imposed upon China by the West (the topic of another book, *Everything Under the Heavens: How the Past Helps Shape China's Push for Global Power* [2017] by Howard W. French), he concludes:

> What is the dynamic process by which either the rule of law or democratic accountability can be expected to spread? This will not happen as a result of top-down mandates by the current leadership, which is brimming with self-confidence and shows little inclination to move on the political front. Change is more likely to occur as new social actors appear on the scene who press for stronger institutions of constraint. In the past, the Chinese state was strong enough to prevent the emergence of powerful social groups that might challenge its power. But social mobilization is occurring in contemporary China at a pace without precedent in all of Chinese history. A huge middle class, currently numbering in the hundreds of millions, has appeared. The future of rule of law and democracy in China will depend on whether these new social groups can shift the classic balance of power between state and society that persisted in China's past. (2015, 385)

Here Fukuyama admits that history has not yet quite ended, but he seems hopeful that it will. Not only has history not ended, but Fukuyama's book has not either. After the previously quoted paragraph, he includes more than 150 pages of text in which he extends his analysis into Africa and the Islamic world, but the point was made by 385 about the development and spread of centralized governments with the rule of law and accountability.

The author concludes his book with prudency. "There is no automatic historical mechanism that makes progress inevitable, or that prevents decay and backsliding. Democracies exist and survive only because people want and are willing to fight for them; leadership, organizational ability, and oftentimes sheer good luck are needed form them to prevail" (2015, 548).

Parts of Fukuyama's analysis are flawed or incomplete, but these are minor compared to the great service he has done for humanity by defining the three major components of good government, analyzing their evolution, and advocating for those principles over other forms of government because they are simply the best principles for people to live under. There is no "Western model" of government and human rights, only a universal model that happened to develop in the West. That understanding should be a good new beginning for world history.

FIVE
World History in Academia and the Development of Big History

World history, because it does not fit well with the traditional historical research model, developed outside of academia and has been shaped largely through works designed to reach a popular market. World history does have a history in academia and education, however, but the field's lack of clear disciplinary boundaries has caused difficulties in defining world history's purpose and has ultimately led to the aberration that is "Big History." "Big History" should be viewed not as a field in itself but as a symptom of larger problems within the development of the world historical field. With those problems diagnosed and cured, so-called Big History should shrink away.

Because this chapter differs from the previous chapters in the sense that no single "work" will be exhaustively analyzed, and because world history's history in education and academia is a big topic, a few disclaimers and parameters must be made:

1. Arnold J. Toynbee's (1889–1975) twelve-volume *A Study of History* (published between 1934 and 1961) was not analyzed in either volume 1 or volume 2 largely because the collection is only tangentially about world history, the real subject being Toynbee's often bizarre theorizing.

    Toynbee enjoyed an academic reputation in the United Kingdom, but his books are impenetrable and seemed to be in fashion for a time only because of how impressive they looked upon the shelf (at a time when that mattered). When scholars actually read the series, they found a little bit of history and a great bit of rambling. Will and Ariel Durant provided a better example of the "multivolume" approach to world history, and they were analyzed

in volume 1. Toynbee does deserve mention, however, because he was the first academic to have the intention of developing a single work of world history and he did act as a mentor to William H. McNeill. (McNeill later wrote a biography about Toynbee.)
2. This chapter will not explore the development of junior high or high school standards regarding world history. At the junior high and high school level, "world history" tends to mean the study of geography and culture outside of the United States and Western Europe. There is nothing wrong with this, of course, but an analysis of state educational standards regarding world history is beyond the scope of this book.
3. Likewise, the development of College Board's Advanced Placement World History course of high schools will not be analyzed here either as to do so would take this volume too far beyond its thesis.
4. This chapter will not be exhaustive, so quite a bit will be left out regarding world historical journals, etc. The purpose of this chapter is to trace the academic process of world history from William J. McNeill to Big History by focusing on a few large-scale works and themes. The goal of the chapter is to clarify what "world history" is and to lead to a concluding chapter that might provide a purpose and future for the field.

William H. McNeill created a place for world history in the world of scholarship in 1967 when his collegiate textbook, simply and appropriately titled *A World History*, was published. In the preface to the fourth edition (1999), McNeill writes:

> A book that remains in print for more than thirty years must have something going for it. Two features of this book probably explain its longevity: 1) a coherent and intelligible account of world history, written from a single, simple point of view, as explained in the Preface; 2) its superior brevity when compared to most other textbooks.
>
> As originally conceived, brevity was imperative, for *A World History*, was initially matched by Readings in World History (10 vols., Oxford University Press 1968–73) with the idea that students of world history might concentrate on studying the human past through such readings, and rely on a suitably short textbook for background and content. In that way, multiple viewpoints could enlarge and enrich the personal vision of the past expressed in these pages, and students could begin to shape their own understanding independently of any single instructor's point of view.
>
> Perhaps this was an over-optimistic vision of what students were willing and able to do. At any rate, few teachers of world history used Readings in World History, so the books soon went out of print, and a projected set of visual sources for world history was never published. Yet this book chugged along in a modest way. (1998, xiii)

The "Readings in World History" set indeed provides an excellent collection of primary documents that range across the world's times and places. Nothing in the collection, or in the fourth edition of *A World History*, indicates that the two are linked in any way. McNeill does not reference the ten volumes in his textbook, for example, which is probably why it works so well as a standalone text.

Unlike most of the other authors of world history who have been analyzed so far, McNeill spent his professional life in the academy; he taught at the University of Chicago starting in 1947 and was there when his breakout book, *The Rise of the West*, was published in 1963. The title of the book indicates that McNeill saw the development of Western Europe as the big change in world history from 1492 to the time of his writing, and the word "rise" is comparative, indicating that the West was somehow once underneath other cultures in terms of global influence.

The Rise of the West was published at a time when McNeill had just risen himself to the rank of History Department Chair at the University of Chicago. *The Rise of the West* won a National Book Award for the category of History and Biography. The National Book Award was the first of a slew of awards and honors that McNeill would accrue over a long life, and he helped to develop academic respectability for the discipline of world history.

A World History is the most symmetrical of any world history ever done. McNeill's reference to "brevity" in the quoted section of the fourth edition's preface might be a bit overstated, however, for a book that includes 552 pages of dense text. The largest challenge in world history comes from arranging the information into a single narrative, one that connects the major events without losing a storytelling thread, and McNeill masters this approach.

What made *A World History* unique for the time was the ability of the author to include factors not typically associated with history in his narrative and explanation. These biological and geographical factors supported a clear focus on the eventual rise of Western Europe while focusing on real historical and geographical reasons why the rest of the world failed to "rise" in relation to the West.

Other historians had focused on factors like crops and disease before, but only for localized descriptions. McNeill connected factors from across disciplines to create a grand theory for how and why Western civilization emerged as the protagonist in world history. Consider this passage regarding the Americas at the time of European conquest and consolidation:

> American crops were botanically altogether different from those familiar in the Old World. Some of them proved to be extremely valuable supplements to what European, Asian, and African farmers had previously known. American corn, or maize, for example, spread rapidly to

southwestern China, Africa, and southeastern Europe. In China the potato proved to be less important than the botanically unrelated sweet potato, which flourished abundantly on hillsides and other previously waste lands, where rice could not be grown. In Europe the relationship was reversed, for a cooler climate suited a plant native to the high Andes, whereas European summers were not warm enough to allow sweet potatoes to mature.

The reception of American food crops increased local food supplies, and usually proved a corresponding increase in population . . .

Details of the American food plant migration are not well established, and it is likely that the major impact of the new crops came after rather than before 1650. This was certainly the case in Europe, where it took time for illiterate cultivators and tradition-bound peasantries to discover the advantages of and to learn how to raise the new crops. (1998, 305–6)

This last paragraph, and particularly the sentence fragment "details of the American food plant migration are not well established," revealed an explanatory gap that needed to be filled. In 1972, Alfred Crosby published his landmark *The Columbian Exchange: Biological and Cultural Consequences of 1492*, which created a whole new understanding about how biological forces can destroy societies and create new epochs in history. More will be said later about Crosby and his work, but for now a few more points must be made about *A World History* by McNeill.

As has been stated before, world history is about Western civilization in the same way that *Hamlet* is about Hamlet. At some point after the 1960s, identity politics began a wave after wave assault on not just the Western literary canon but also on any historical studies that focused on the development and achievements of Western civilization. McNeill thought and wrote before this movement and he continues with his "rise of the west" theme throughout *A World History*. Consider this extract:

> No other civilization responded to the new possibilities opened by ocean travel with anything remotely resembling European venturesomeness. Toying with foreign novelties did occur, most notably in the Far East, but nothing inimical to ancient and well-established tradition ruffled the mind of Chinese mandarins for very long. Moslem and Hindu reaction was even more emphatically negative. Anything conflicting with ancient truths was simply repudiated and neglected—or not noticed at all.
>
> How different was Europe's response, where the convulsions of the Age of Renaissance and Reformation shook European society to its core and shattered the medieval frame of European civilization entirely! The stimulus of the discoveries, and their subsequent exploitation, was not the sole cause of this transformation of Europe. Deep-seated and long-standing tensions with European civilization contributed at least as much as anything from the outside. (1998, 308)

McNeill is right; to study Chinese civilization is to study centuries of politics that were dominated by boring and repressive test takers like the Confucian bureaucrats. The Chinese bureaucracy certainly developed impressive feats of engineering, but they also ignored innovative practices and butchered the feet of their women. The exclamation point that McNeill employs (rare for a world history textbook) reveals the unapologetic excitement that comes from studying Western civilization in her period of transformation and dynamism.

One paragraph about Western civilization needs to be included here not because McNeill did anything exceptionally new with it but because it reveals his dry wit:

> The English Civil Wars (1642–48) also ran counter to the trend toward monarchical absolutism. It was the parliamentary opponents of modern, efficient royal bureaucracy who prevailed. Like the Reformation itself, the parliamentary cause was radically reactionary, for it rested both on a reaffirmation of the traditional liberties of Englishmen (Magna Carta and all that) and upon relentless Puritanical striving after a government of saints. (1998, 312)

The parenthetical reference is both an eye roll regarding the traditional Magna Carta to American Constitution timeline that legal scholars are so proud of and a wink at the reader. This mastery of traditional historical content is written right along with new insights about the role of disease in the European consolidation of the New World as the Spanish developed a silver mining empire based on coercive labor:

> The mines, too, whence came the flow of silver that so disturbed the world's price system, were promptly organized along European technical lines. But the great peasant majority at first lived much as before. The new masters with their religion and laws played the same limited role in their lives that the vanished rulers of the Aztec and Inca past had done. This simple relationship was soon upset by the fact . . . that diseases cut deeply into village manpower. As depopulation proceeded, the old subsistence agriculture broke down, for the Spaniards badly needed the village labor that did remain to feed the towns and to work in the mines. To be sure, Spanish law did not permit enslavement, and official policy, as laid down in Madrid, protected Indian rights very thoroughly. All the same, the needs of Spanish settlers came first, and when they required Indian labor they got it, usually by allowing the Indians to incur debts and then enforcing a creditor's perfectly legal rights against insolvent debtors. Such debts became hereditary; and Indian debtors were put to work under the direction of the Spanish settlers to perform whatever tasks the Spaniards needed done. (1998, 334)

Here McNeill describes for the reader the effects of the disease epidemics that destroyed native populations, but he does not give geographical/biological reasons as to why the Europeans brought the diseases that the natives died of, rather than vice versa. He also does not ask the question that later became rather popular among historians, that of "why didn't Native Americans sail east across the Atlantic and settle Europe?" That's a question with answers that only lie in deep history, but it would create another phase in world historical studies.

From McNeill, world history branches off into three distinct phases: 1) world history that abandons the "to explain it all" conceit and focuses a comparative analysis of different eras and regions of the world, with geology, biology, and politics seen as key historical driving factors (this becomes very popular); 2) world history's evolution into "Big History"; and 3) world history for educational purposes, as a means of gaining an understanding of broad historical connections and for developing cross-curricular thought patterns. These categories are loose but provide some framework for understanding and will now be included as subcategories. Because the third category involves this author's previous works in the field, the third will be analyzed in the conclusion.

WORLD HISTORY AS COMPARATIVE ANALYSIS

McNeill's *A World History* referenced the food and disease exchanges that took place as a result of the European conquest of the new world. McNeill's textbook is the most symmetrical world history in existence, and he wrote about food and disease with the same level of succinctness that he applied to more traditional world historical topics like the Chinese dynasties. Still, McNeill's mention of biological material as a major historical factor seemed to open up an entirely new branch of study that deserved a deeper historical analysis: enter Alfred Crosby (1931–2018).

Crosby never wrote a full-scale world history, but he seemed fascinated by the post-1492 period and the development of a new Western civilization. McNeill's genius was more conservative, and his work *A World History* seemed like something that a traditional historian could read and appreciate. McNeill's work indicates that he saw the field of world history as a survey of times and places and perhaps as a framework that would enhance one's understanding of more traditional historical topics. The best evidence for this point comes from reading the website of the University of Chicago's History Department—not one of the professors in the department is specialist in "world history"; all are specialists in specific and traditional fields.

Crosby's obituary mentioned that it took the author three years to find a press for his manuscript and that over twenty different presses rejected it before a small press finally decided to publish (and Crosby was a Harvard graduate with excellent academic credentials). Crosby's difficulty in publishing probably was a result of his new cross-curricular approach, making it difficult to categorize his work, and this offers more proof for how uncomfortable academia has traditionally been with world history as a subject.

However, the force of his argument, that the voyages of Columbus created the most cataclysmic plague in history for the natives while entirely altering the New World into something more like Europe, was so impressive that Crosby's contribution could not be ignored and the phrase "Columbian Exchange" gradually developed into a core concept of traditional historical studies.

Crosby followed up *The Columbian Exchange* with four books on ecological and epidemiological history, including a 1986 work titled *Ecological Imperialism: The Biological Expansion of Europe, 900–1900*, and this work, maybe even more than *The Columbian Exchange*, connected the fields of biology and history.

In *Ecological Imperialism*, Crosby referred to the Americas, South Africa, and Australia as "neo-Europes" in the sense that European explorers were able to transform those regions by bringing in livestock, invasive plant species, and even honeybees into extensions of the European homeland. With Crosby's biography in mind, we now need to link to the years 1997 and 1998, which saw the publication of three critical books, none of which were world histories and all of which employed or argued for a cross-curricular methodology.

What's most interesting about Crosby's work in biological history is that it is not even the most interesting work he produced. His 1997 book, *The Measure of Reality: Quantification and Western Society, 1250–1600*, begins with "Pantometry: An Introduction," and this is where Crosby introduces the concept of a society's entire ability to measure things. The introduction includes a discussion about medieval Western Europe and her intellectual position as it related to the Islamic world both before and after the process of quantification. Crosby discusses Plato and Aristotle in terms of how they quantified materials around them. Then he writes:

> We would claim that weight, hardness, and temperature "and other sensible contrarieties" are quantifiable, but that is not implicit either in these qualities or in the nature of the human mind. Our child psychologists declare that humans, even in infancy, show indications that they are innately endowed with the ability to count discrete entities (three cookies, six balls, eight pigs), but weight, hardness, and so on do not come to us as quantities of discrete entities. They are conditions, not collections; and, even worse, they are often flowing changes. We cannot count them as they are; we have to see them with our mind's eye, quantify them by fiat, and then count the quanta. That is easily done with measuring extension—for example, this lance is so many feet long, and we can count them by laying the lance on the ground and mincing along its length. But hardness, heat, speed, acceleration—how in the world would we quantify those? (1997, 13)

With a paragraph like that, Crosby inaugurates a new phase of world historical studies. He's not trying to "explain it all," but like James Burke in his 1987 work *The Day the Universe Changed*, Crosby seems interested in understanding how the human schema for understanding the world shifted. Crosby begins by describing "the Venerable model" of how early medieval people quantified the world and then explains how several historical factors must sometimes come together at once in order for a societal and mental shift to occur.

Chapter 3, "Necessary but Insufficient Causes," begins with a 1981 quote from William Reese: "In causal terms the presence of oxygen is a necessary but not a sufficient condition for fire. Oxygen plus combustibles plus the striking of a match would illustrate a sufficient condition for fire" (1997, 49). If fire needs three causes, then think how many the Protestant Reformation needed! This insight about necessary but insufficient causes creates a new framework for studying world historical movements.

The chapter on time includes this shocking thought: Westerners quantified time by equating it to space. Crosby does not explain it this way, but if you look at a clock and you look at a ruler, you will see that they are the same. The clock is a ruler bent into a circle, and quantified time means that the clock is measuring something. (Crosby does not state this, but the clock measures movement, which is why when there is no movement there is no time, hence the t=0 equation that physicists know represents the pre-universe and the fact that your relation to time depends on your speed in the same way that your relation to distance does.)

Space, visualization, music, and painting are all treated as subsections to a new European passion for quantification and new forms of mathematical analysis. The final chapter before the epilogue is titled "Bookkeeping," and Crosby explains how the simple concept of double entry bookkeeping, in which one column is used to keep track of what a person spent and another column is used to keep track of what someone made, imposed order on a chaotic late medieval economy:

> About 1300, in that wondrous era of eyeglasses, clocks, *ars nova*, and Giotto, some Italian accountants began using what we call double-entry bookkeeping. Possibly, in its origins, it had some relationship with algebra (from the Arabic *al-jabr*, and not by accident), which also divides the grist that comes to its mill into two categories, insisting that what is plus in one column can be only minus in the other, and vice versa. What we do know is that at the beginning of the fourteenth century Rinieri Fini, agent of a Florentine banking house at the fairs in Champagne, and Tuscan merchants working out of Nimes in the south of France were keeping their books with assets and liabilities posted separately. This was just a beginning; yet to come were a number of features of technical language, abbreviation, and form that we consider characteristic of and even essential to bookkeeping. (1997, 206)

Double entry bookkeeping would later make it possible for the Western European economy to digest all the Latin American gold and silver that flowed into the continent after the time of Columbus. The modern stock market, in some ways, is just an elaboration on the system of double entry bookkeeping. If all that Crosby had done was fascinate readers with the origins of our measurement systems, he would have contributed greatly to world historical studies. But he does not stop with a traditional historical research. He works his way into the history of quantification and, regarding the moment when "Arabic" (actually Indian) numerals arrived in the West, he writes:

> Mathematics was not ready for swift advance. Its symbols and techniques were inadequate. The moment had arrived for a trumpet solo, and the only instrument available was a hunting horn. Furthermore, mathematics was not, in a manner of speaking, homogenously equal to homogenous time and space. Numbers and concepts were still resonating with nonmathematical significance. Yes, 3 was 1 plus 1 plus 1 or the square root of 9, and so on, but it was also at unpredictable moments a direct reference to the Trinity.
>
> But let us deal first with getting from the hunting horn to the trumpet. Let us look at counting, arithmetic, and simple algebra . . . counting, especially if the numbers got high, was very difficult in Roman numerals. . . . Complicated computation with Roman numerals was impractical, if not impossible, and the mixing and confusion of numbers and letters were hard to avoid, because, of course, Roman numerals were Roman letters. (1997, 111)

If you follow this analogy, it leads you right into an epistemological wilderness. If at one time thinkers in Western Europe found themselves confronted by problems that Roman numerals could not solve, then this raises the notion the problems inherent in modern theoretical physics may not be solvable with our current mathematical instruments. Have we reached the limits of what the symbols 0 through 9 and the variations of add, subtract, multiply, and divide can do? Do we need new symbols and entirely new forms of thought in order to solve the deepest problems in physics?

Reading Crosby in the modern era is probably analogous to reading Francis Bacon in the seventeenth century. Bacon detailed scientific experimentation and the accumulation of evidence to be the "new method, or new organ" (*Novum Organum* in Latin) over the old method of studying the ancients. Appropriately, the last chapter of *The Measure of Reality* is titled "The New Model." Crosby was writing about and old new model while employing cross-curricular intellectual methods that were helping to create a new one.

Crosby's genius was predicated on the notion that something special happened in Western Europe between 1250 and 1600 that did not occur anywhere else in the world. It's not clear that such assertions could be made in an early twenty-first-century academic environment, and, as this volume shows, the trend in world historical approaches has veered away from Eurocentrism. These alternative approaches offer much less than the Eurocentric approach in terms of intellectual discovery. The study of China or Africa between 1250 and 1600 does not yield the kinds of insights that the study of Europe does.

As can be seen from these quotes, Crosby's writing style and eclectic choice of topics prevented some scholars from appreciating his work. For most of these two volumes, the biographies of the world history writers have been largely omitted except when facts are relevant to the topic of the approach, but it must be noted here that McNeill died in 2016 and Crosby just two years later.

While both men were chairs of history departments, the University of Chicago for McNeill and the University of Texas, Austin, for Crosby, McNeill was laden with honors throughout his career, including a National Book Award for *The Rise of the West* and a National Humanities Medal in 2009. Crosby received academic fellowships, including a Guggenheim, but not the same level of acclaim as McNeill. Crosby's work simply seemed to fall outside of the traditional modes of historical scholarship, and the difficulty he faced in finding publication for *The Columbian Exchange* and the relative lack of recognition for his work speak to how uneasy the academic world has been with the cross-disciplinary world historical approach.

Despite the fact that the phrase "the Columbian Exchange" entered the historical lexicon, Crosby's work never entered into the mainstream consciousness. Neither, it should be added, did McNeill's. McNeill and Crosby were rogue academics, which probably explains why a niche was left open for the arrival of a popular book of cross-curricular synthesis.

Jared Diamond's *Guns, Germs, and Steel: The Fates of Human Societies* differed from Crosby's work on ecological history for a few reasons. First, Diamond wrote explicitly that one of his reasons for writing was to fully repudiate a racist history and to replace racial explanations of world historical development with geographic explanations. Second, Crosby phrased his big question as, to paraphrase, "Why did the societies of the West have so much 'cargo' (technological stuff, as phrased by an indigenous friend of his) while the people of, say, Papua New Guinea possessed so little?" Diamond put forth geography, with the east-west axis of Eurasia, as the primary answer.

Like the phrase "Columbian Exchange," the phrase "Guns, Germs, and Steel" made its way into the world historical lexicon. Diamond himself is an example of the kind of polymath, like H. G. Wells, who is attracted to the cross-discipline nature of world history. Like so many thinkers in the discipline, Diamond came to the study of world history from an unusual background. He had been a physician and world-renowned expert on the gall bladder before winning a MacArthur Genius grant in 1985, which allowed him to pursue his larger academic interests (going from the gall bladder to the biggest questions in world historical study is quite a leap!).

Diamond's 1997 book won the Pulitzer Prize, but it was another book published that year that made a call for cross-curricular study. A year after *Guns, Germs, and Steel* was published, the famed etymologist and all-around genius Edward O. Wilson published *Consilience: The Unity of Knowledge*. World history as a cross-curricular enterprise had begun when historians began to delve into biology as a factor, but now the biologists (Diamond and Wilson) were writing histories, or philosophies based on history, and shaping the thought process in an opposite way.

In *Consilience*, Wilson urged philosophers to think in a cross-curricular manner based on an understanding that knowledge cannot necessarily be sliced up into discrete subjects. He wrote:

> The greatest enterprise of the mind has always been and always will be the attempted linkage of the sciences and the humanities. The ongoing fragmentation of knowledge and resulting chaos in philosophy are not reflections of the real world but artifacts of scholarship. The proposition of the original Enlightenment are increasingly favored by objective evidence, especially from the natural sciences.
> Consilience is the key to unification. (1998, 9)

By consilience, Wilson means that a unifying theoretical principle can be derived from differing data sets. One could study DNA evidence, bones from frogs or birds, or even the history of cell phones and derive the theory of evolution from analyzing all of them. A scientific theory derived from differing data sets begins inductively and, at some point, when it proves useful in a consistent way, it gets applied deductively to new phenomena. Increasingly, world history seemed to be the most likely candidate for disciplines to converge and unify.

The year 1998 also saw the publication of William McNeill's *Plagues and Peoples* about the effects of disease in world history. Then William McNeill, with his son (an accomplished academic himself) J. R. McNeill, had a new world history titled *The Human Web: A Bird's Eye View of World History*, published in 2003. The book was an attempt to shorten his earlier work while providing an updated form of scholarship including the new insights that had developed since *A World History* had been published in 1967. McNeill and his son employed a "web" analogy, explaining how Old World webs formed as a result of trade and conquest and then expanded to include the rest of the world.

A World History was published just a few years after the birth control pill became publicly available, and demography emerged as an important subject in the twentieth century. The McNeills highlight the importance of population growth in the eighteenth century:

136   *Chapter 5*

> China's population doubled, and Europe's almost did so. In the Americas, population grew even faster, rebounding from the disasters that had followed the linkup to the Old World Web. Evidence is sparse for India and Africa, but their growth apparently lagged behind the pace set by China and Europe. The world's total by 1800 was probably around 900 million. Population growth in the 1700s reached 30 percent per century, nearly three times as fast as in the centuries before 1700. Epidemics and famines did not disappear, but they became less frequent and less severe. By 1900, world population had reached 1.6 billion, a growth rate of nearly 80 percent per century. A fundamental transition was underway. (1998, 222)

There is also a subsection titled "Ecological Change" that includes these sentences:

> The tightening web carried plants, animals, and diseases around the world too, although with less revolutionary results than in the wake of Columbus. American food crops continued their spread throughout Africa and Eurasia. In one corner of Tanzania, by the late 1800s about one of every three cultivated plants was American in origin. Maize probably had its biggest impact on China in the eighteenth and nineteenth centuries. Simultaneously, Old World food crops extended their colonization of the Americas, notably wheat on the former grasslands of the prairies and Pampas. The Columbian Exchange continued to bring Old World pathogens to new groups of Amerindians thought the eighteenth and nineteenth centuries. (1998, 265)

How delightful it is to read these words and realize that the old scholar McNeill was still capable of reinterpreting world history through the work of new scholarship at this stage of his life. It's not just that the McNeills added a few sentences to a previous thesis either.

The entire "web" analogy seems derived from the work of Crosby and Diamond. *The Human Web* is a brilliant book and probably would be the best starter book for anyone new to world history and global studies, but chapter 9, in which first J. R. and then William write their concluding words, signals the earliest movement toward "Big History."

J. R. McNeill writes:

> The universe, soon after it exploded in the Big Bang roughly 12 billion years ago, began to acquire islands of order, structure, and complexity such as galaxies, stars, and planets. These were created by flows of gravitational energy, and maintain their structure, their complexity, by further flows of energy. Stars, for example, were created by gravitational pulls on dust and gas. They evolved structures and gradients so that particles and heat move around within them in regular fashion. But eventually they scatter (by exuding heat) so much of the energy they captured that they collapse and die. They can attain and maintain order only by capturing and using energy, and they cannot keep it up forever.

> Living organisms, whether single-celled life or giraffes, follow approximately the same script. (2003, 319–20)

J. R.'s father, in his concluding section, picks up on this idea and writes:

> The human record conforms to larger evolutionary patterns. Exact and surprising parallels can, in fact, be surmised in the deep past, when bacteria first formed innumerable living cells in the earth's oceans, and sporadically exchanged genetic material by direct contact of one to another in much the same way that early human bands exchanged information by meeting and mingling together on festival occasions. Time and again, direct bacterial genetic exchange had the effect of permitting cells to propagate useful mutations and so adapt to altering environmental circumstances. (2003, 324)

That such proclamations occur at the end, rather than the beginning, of their book is revealing. The McNeills seemed unready to work such thoughts into a grander thesis that would connect the "Big Bang" to microbial evolution, to the evolution of humans, and eventually to the creation of societies and "human webs." They were right to be reticent. Nonetheless, the origins of a new approach can be found in *The Human Web* and, in particular, in the concluding paragraphs.

Enter David Christian and his "Big History" approach.

BIG HISTORY

McNeill wrote in his introduction to Christian's 2004 book *Maps of Time: An Introduction to Big History*, a book that, in McNeill's words, "unites natural history and human history in a single, grand, and intelligible narrative" (2005, xv). McNeill achieved great things, but a sentence like that shows why historians should stay away from theoretical physics.

Although Big History's problems will soon be written out in detail, McNeill's statement must be dealt with right away. The universe has no single past and therefore no single narrative, only probable pasts that are analyzed based on the limited knowledge that scientists have in the present.

The Big Bang is unlikely as an origin event, however, because entropy is at the core of everything in the universe, and even high-gravity singularities like black holes radiate because of decay rather than explode. What if the universe began with a Slow Drip in an environment where modern forms of time analysis had no meaning?

Christian's attempt to unite all fields into a single narrative, "Big History," has does have one virtue: the approach allows for the skipping over of problematic early world historical sources, such as Herodotus, in favor of a larger-scale view of history in epochal chunks. Christian, who was born in 1946, first made his career as a traditional historian in the field of Russian and Soviet studies.

After the collapse of the Soviet system, Christian seems to have redirected his interests into Big History. Christian has written several books and given a Great Courses lecture series on his approach; most of these works are reiterations on the same theme. Christian has acquired a few acolytes, so there are other authors working in the Big History genre. Christian's prolific output, three books and the lecture series, and the output of other writers bring up a question: wasn't "Big History" supposed to be about the creation of a single narrative? If so, what can a new book be but a rewriting of the past book?

Christian's first book on Big History was the aforementioned *Maps of Time*, and his most recent work was *Origin Story: A Big History of Everything* (2018). Big History has become more of an enterprise than an approach and in the preface to the 2011 edition of *Maps of Time*, Christian writes: "Since 2004 there have been major organizational developments in the field. The number of college-level courses in big history has increased rapidly, and there may be at least fifty such courses being taught throughout the world today. . . . In April 2011, a scholarly organization was founded to develop big history as a research and teaching field: the International Big History Association" (xxv).

No single book serves as a representative of the approach, and Christian is not writing a multivolume work so much as he is just restating a single point in different ways and then adding more cut and paste science to his narrative.

It's not clear what "big history as a research and teaching field," to use Christian's phrase, means. How does one conduct research in Big History when the point of the "field" seems to be to incorporate research from other traditional fields into the narrative? When a Big History writer cuts and pastes the research of others, nothing is earned and misunderstandings occur. For example, in *Maps of Time*, Christian, attempting to explain the early universe, quotes both a Mayan manuscript and a Zen teaching, then writes:

> One of the trickiest problems concerns time. Was there a "time" when there was no time? Is time a product of our imagination? In some systems of thought, time does not really exist. Places become the source of everything significant, and the paradoxes of creation take different forms. But for communities that see time as central, there is no way of avoiding the paradox of origins. (2005, 19)

"Time" really is not that complicated, and there is nothing mystical about it. Look at a ruler and look at a clock and you will see that a clock is just a ruler bent into a circle. Rulers measure distance, but what does a clock measure? The answer is that a clock measures movement. Movement in the real world comes chaotically, but clocks keep a consistent movement that is useful for human schedules.

Seeing time as a measure of movement solves all of the big paradoxes and questions: 1) The absence of movement equals the absence of time. Theoretical physicists use the equation $t=0$ to show that no movement and therefore no time exists. (Real time, as opposed to Platonic time, is really measured in temperature, which details the actual level movement of the specific object.) 2) In the same way that speed of movement alters a person's perception of distance, it also alters our perception of movement; this is at the core of Relativity Theory. 3) "Time travel" in the conventional sense is not possible because time is just the reorganization of matter into different forms. You can't go back and kill your grandfather, for example, because you were there when your grandfather was alive; you just weren't you.

If time is the measurement of motion, one might ask how much motion is required to create time. The answer to that depends on what kind of measurement device one is using. An observation of any kind is defined as a synthesis between the observer and the thing observed. Undetectable motion is not motion for a human observer.

Christian did not earn his statement about time by actually studying theoretical models, so instead the reader receives evasions. One more example will serve for many other tiresome examples. Christian is not a cosmologist or a theoretical physicist and so, in justifying a reverence for the Big Bang, he writes about Edwin Hubble:

> Hubble also . . . showed that by measuring the rate of expansion, scientists should be able to estimate how long the universe has been expanding. This was an astonishing conclusion, for it seemed to imply something totally unexpected. Hubble had found a way of measuring the age of the universe! Originally, he calculated that the rate of expansion (or the Hubble constant) was ca. 500 kilometers per second for every megaparsec of distance between two objects. (A megaparsec is the distance traveled by light in 3.26 million years . . .) This figure meant that the universe could only be about two billion years old. We now known that this is an impossible date, as the earth itself is at least twice this age. Modern estimates of the Hubble constant are lower, and imply an older universe. But determining exactly how old remains tricky, mainly because of the difficulty of calculating the real distance of remote galaxies. Modern attempts, which use several other types of distance markers in addition to Cepheid variables, suggest that the Hubble constant lies between 55 and 75 km per second per megaparsec. These figures imply that the universe is between 10 and 16 billion years old, and the most recent estimates seem to be converging on a figure of about 13 billion years. (2005, 31–32)

Christian's conceptual error gets shared across the Big History spectrum. The David Christian book titled *Big History: Examines Our Past, Explains Our Present, Imagines our Future* includes this sentence in a timeline: "13.8 BYA: The Universe Forms in the Big Bang." The "BYA" stands for billion years ago. What exactly does "billion years ago" mean in this context? We would have to imagine an Earth spinning around the sun at its current rate and then put that concept out in a Platonic realm and imagine going back to a state in time that included neither the sun nor the Earth. Then we would need to further imagine that the early universe's gravitation had no effect on the spinning of our Platonic sun-Earth combination.

From this, Christian's approach includes cell biology, etc. (secondary accounts of biology) and eventually the development of human societies. Perhaps because his first book seemed to stray so far from traditional world history, Christian summarized the human history of *Maps of Time* in *This Fleeting World: A Short History of Humanity* in 2007. Nothing really new appears in this volume; it's a Cliff's Notes version of *Maps of Time*, but the introduction is written by Bob Bain and Lauren MacArthur Harris, both of the University of Michigan.

Both Bain and Harris, the preface notes, "are former high school world history teachers with over thirty-five years of combine experience." The choice of preface authors, plus an endorsement from a "College Board Consultant for AP World History," indicates that *This Fleeting World* might have been meant as a supplement to frame the AP World History course.

A curiosity about both *This Fleeting World* and Christian's next book *Origin Story* is that both feature an endorsing quote from Bill Gates on the covers. Publishers can hardly be blamed for trying to grab the attention of book buyers by including the name of a rich and famous endorser on the covers, but a skeptic might ask why the opinion of Bill Gates matters at all regarding a book about science and history. Gates is not recognized as an expert in anything other than making money from word processors and then using that money to help improve conditions in developing countries.

This Fleeting World contains only ninety-two pages of text and divides human history into just three major epochs: 1) "The Era of Foragers," 2) "Acceleration: The Agrarian Era," and 3) "Our World: The Modern Era." *This Fleeting World* resembles a wiki summary of global events. Occasional "thought experiment" inserts trivialize the practice of world history, such as:

> In 1945, President Harry Truman decided to use the atomic bomb to end World War II in the Pacific. Consider that ever since people have debated Truman's decision to use this most terrible weapon and that more and more countries have "joined" the nuclear club. Now imagine you could advise Truman, knowing what you know now. Would you suggest other options? Do you think it is significant that the United States remains the only country in the world to have used nuclear weapons in combat? (2008, 79)

Even if one plays within the absurdity of this scenario, the only appropriate answer is to advise Truman to do exactly what he did. Not only did the atomic weapons put an end to four decades of Japanese terror in the Pacific, but the bombs saved American (and Japanese) lives and predicated the transformation of Japan into a free society with one of the best functioning economies in the world. None of this is to downplay or disrespect the damage that the bombs caused to real people in Hiroshima and Nagasaki, but to even suggest that Truman's decision was ill advised speaks to a major problem with this methodology.

Big History may eventually be world history's version of string theory. Peter Woit, in 2010, wrote *Not Even Wrong: The Failure of String Theory and the Continuing Challenge to Unify the Laws of Physics* and made the argument that string theory, by trying to unite disciplines, developed such a convoluted set of theories and explanations that it really made no testable assertions at all. Big History too is not even wrong (except when, as has been shown in the case of the secondhand physics that Christian includes, it's just wrong) in the sense that it makes no real assertions about history. The creativity involved in Big History seems to be in the development of clever categorizations. For example, *Origin Story* is divided into four parts: 1) Cosmos, 2) Biosphere, 3) Us, and 4) The Future. The subcategories come in "thresholds" such as chapter 2, "Stars and Galaxies: Thresholds 2 and 3."

Nothing new gets said in these pages. Christian's enterprise is similar to that of a medieval monk laboring in a scriptorium in that he is translating the work of other hands and minds and illustrating them with clever subheadings and analogies such as "the spooky thing about life is that, though the inside of each cell looks like a pandemonium—a sort of mud-wrestling contest involving a million molecules—whole cells give the impression of acting with purpose" (2008, 76). This stands for the whole book; it's a generalized statement that stays far enough from actual biology to be safe, and the mud wrestling reference keeps the paragraph from appearing too intellectual. (Christian's writing style frequently frustrates a literate reader; in this example, he sets the paragraph up with the word "spooky" then moves to a very nonspooky mud wrestling metaphor.)

The Big History approach to world history not only fails but does violence to the purpose of world history, which should be to impart upon the student a set of thought processes that can prove to be useful in the development of cross-curricular analogies. Christian wants a single narrative to be taught to potential disciples from the top down. What's the purpose? It's not clear how practitioners can add to a field that proposes to be complete. Big History contains very little traditional history; one can read entire books on the topic and not really come away with any new facts or even insights beyond a sense of historical categorization.

In the final section of *Origin Story*, part 4, "The Future," Christian writes a chapter titled "Where Is It All Going?" Despite the sexiness of these titles, Christian's writing style fails to inspire:

> For us humans, the next hundred years are really important. Things are happening so fast that, like the slow-motion time of a near accident, the details of what we do in the next few decades will have huge consequences for us and the biosphere on scales of thousands of years. Like it or not, we are now managing an entire biosphere, and we can do it well or badly. (2018, 289)

An idealistic college freshman could have written that paragraph, and Christian seems to indicate that the purpose of Big History is to understand that the next epoch, or "threshold" or whatever, will involve a sort of green socialism he calls a "mature Anthropocene." Although Christian uses a lot of qualifiers, he finally comes out with his vision:

> Population growth will slow, eventually, to zero, and perhaps start falling. Rates of population growth are already falling in most parts of the world, and in some regions, the absolute number of people is beginning to fall. There are many steps that could speed the process, including better health care for poor families and better education for women and girls in poorer countries. Many economics warn about the danger of slowing population growth, but a biospheric perspective shows why continued population growth is unsustainable. In a mature Anthropocene, poverty will be largely eliminated by better welfare systems and checks on the accumulation of extreme wealth. (2018, 298)

It goes on like this, in tedious detail, with Christian never missing an opportunity to use "many" as his favorite word. There you have it, reader, Big History leads us to the necessity of a mildly liberal global agenda. Big History contains no real history and no real ideas, just the safe notion that no one really needs to know anything but big picture categories and that we can all be safe in knowing that a mastery of such a framework will lead us to a comfortable political ideology. Big History is neither big nor a history, just another pop theory that shrinks away from the light of skeptical analysis.

Conclusion

World History for Education and Analogical Thinking

WORLD HISTORY FOR CROSS-CURRICULAR STUDY

The third branch to come from McNeill involves the use of world history for the purpose of developing analogical thought patterns, and this branch has sub-branches that use the facts of world history to prove theses. Yes, I wrote a world history myself. In the 2015, Rowman & Littlefield published my five-volume series, collectively titled Connecting the Dots in World History: A Teacher's Literacy-Based Curriculum. The title held three specific purposes, the first being the "connect the dots" metaphor, which serves to provide a framework for the development of world history and as an analogy for how to combine the study of world history with learning theory.

In a connect the dots activity, the participant is presented with a seemingly random set of dots and then is given instructions on how to connect those dots until a bigger picture emerges. This metaphor fits well with narrative learning theory in that each chapter is divided into "dots" that are short enough for classroom use but that never lose the narrative connection that is so crucial to the study of world history.

The most important word in the title is "A" as it serves the same purpose that the word "A" did in McNeill's 1967 *A World History*. That single letter shows the humility in the telling of this grand story; there are other ways to tell it, but here's one way.

The "literacy-based curriculum" part of the title indicates that the development of student literacy skills is a prime focus of the book. Research into learning theory indicates that people learn content and develop literacy 1) when contents are written in a narrative form and 2) when the facts connect to other forms of information. One objective of the books was to encourage other teaches to develop their own curricula and to break away from the ineffective textbook and workbook materials that drain so much of the finances of public education while also draining the enjoyment of learning from the classroom.

Even though those five volumes were designed for use in a secondary or collegiate classroom, they are a world history and contain a narrative developed with an overarching explanatory theory. Reviewers uniformly ignored the books, and, aside from a two-part webinar series I conducted on the methodology through the National Council for Social Studies, the impact of the theory and content of those books on the academic community has been minimal.

Most world histories, especially the "big histories," theorize so far from the actual events of history that the impact of actual people, like Suleyman the Magnificent, Phillis Wheatley, and Napoleon Bonaparte, get left out. World history cannot just be a catalog of events within a theoretical framework, not if anyone is going to be interested in it. The connect the dots series was written with the intent of returning the drama of human engagement to the narrative.

The purpose of studying world history should not be to "explain it all" but to help develop cross-curricular analogies that are at the stuff of higher level thought. The human mind, and therefore history, is driven by the development of analogies. Douglas Hofstadter, David Wootton, and A. C. Grayling have all written about the importance of analogy making in the development of science. Wootton, in particular, has written that concept of "discovery," so critical to science, first developed with Columbus and then transferred over into the idea of research.

From the 1990s to the present, E. O. Wilson, Peter Watson, and others have revived the Enlightenment dream of connecting all knowledge into a single discipline. World history became more popular than ever as a source of knowledge and novel insights, but the big schools of thought that came from world historical studies branched into different directions, and most did not try to "explain it all." Still, as this second volume concludes, a few broad categories will be established here regarding some of world history's broader trends beyond the "to explain it all" categories.

The Geographic Determinist School

This includes Alfred Crosby, Jared Diamond, and Peter Watson (Watson's superlative *The Great Divide: Nature and Human Nature in the Old World and the New* [2013] was not mentioned before here, but it is insightful and readable). Crosby, Diamond, and Watson tend to view Earth as a series of geographically discrete petri dishes, where humans, their biospheres, and their ideas interacted separately until people from one of those regions (Europe as a subsection of Eurasia) developed enough technology to connect the world.

The Good News School

Francis Fukayama, Steven Pinker, and Michael Shermer have all written, and not sheepishly, that life for humans is getting rather better. Fukuyama celebrated the collapse of the Soviet state and has written extensively that representative democracy with accountable government remains the "goal" of politics. Pinker, in *The Better Angels of Our Nature: Why Violence Has Declined* (2015) and Shermer with *The Moral Arc: How Science Makes Us Better People* (2016) both use the facts of world history to argue that life now is better than it ever has been. They are all three correct in their assertions, and one day their books will be considered the canon of a new Enlightenment.

Why Nations Fail: The Origins of Power, Prosperity, and Poverty (2012) by Daron Acemoglu and James A. Robinson uses an Adam Smith style of comparative analysis to conclude that nations with "extractive" governments fare worse than those with "inclusive" governments. The authors oversimplify (maybe even mangle) Jared Diamond's thesis, but their book showcases two factors about world history. The authors brilliantly develop a comparative analysis to prove that democratic institutions, being inclusive, factually do a better job at making the lives of real people better than extractive institutions do.

The Education/Consilience School (World History as the Unification of Knowledge)

This began with Wilson's 1994 *Consilience: The Unification of Knowledge* in which Wilson argues for a field that is all the fields. Peter Watson belongs in this school as well as the geographic determinist school because of his book *Convergence: The Idea at the Heart of Science* (2017) in which he argues that nineteenth-century science was shaped by the development of cross-disciplinary connections. Unfortunately, Watson repeatedly argues that Big History will be the nexus of this conversion. Before either of them, McNeill wrote *A World History* primarily for an academic course and his work blended into David Christian's work. Another writer in this field is me, and, at this point, I must explain my own attempt to "explain it all."

World history is the field for polymaths, for thinkers who prefer not to be constrained by the boundaries of a specific research discipline. It should be a process, not a method, an educational practice rather than a singular narrative.

What, a reader might ask, are the suggestions that I might make after all these years of reading and study in world history regarding the narration of the subject? To answer that in the appropriate detail would be essentially to write another book or a long chapter that would divert from this volume's purpose. In short, world historians still tend to miss the major movements.

For example, almost every world historian notes the importance of the printing press for transforming Europe in the fifteenth century, but very few mention that the Ottoman Empire banned the press about the same time. Almost no one, save for myself, has written about how after the Protestant Reformation broke Christendom in 1517, a new West was re-created in 1687 and 1688. These are the years, respectively, when Newton's *Principia* was published and when England became a parliamentary monarchy. The twin pillars of the modern West, science and democracy, were both erected at the same place and the same time.

Still, we miss, over and over again, the real implications of world historical movements. We write of an Enlightenment, an American Declaration of Independence, an American Constitution, a French Revolution, and so forth, but the most impactful event of the eighteenth century surely came when Mary Wollstonecraft published her feminist manifesto *Vindication of the Rights of Women* in 1792. Likewise for the 1848 Seneca Falls Convention. The single most important piece of twentieth-century legislation (if a dictatorial decree can be called that) came when Mao Zedong banned female foot binding. Enlightenment values unleashed feminism first and then created constitutions and the rule of the law second, to put things in their proper order of importance. Perhaps *A Skeptic's History of the World* is needed, one that will reexamine the assumptions at the core of the field.

No single narrative or approach can ever "explain it all," but world history remains the best place for thinkers to develop cross-curricular analogies, and that means that world history is most useful as an educational tool. It is the only subject for polymaths rather than specialists. Instead of trying to create a single narrative to be presented to students and the public from the top down, world history should be a flexible discipline that allows for cross-curricular thinkers to see connections across disciplines from the bottom up. World history would then be what it has always been, the perfect subject for people who are interested in all the subjects.

References

Acemoglu, Daron, and James A. Robinson. 2012. *Why Nations Fail: The Origins of Power, Prosperity, and Poverty*. New York: Random House.
Ansary, Tamim. (2009) 2010. *Destiny Disrupted: A History of the World through Islamic Eyes*. New York: Public Affairs Reprint.
Booth, Mark. (2007) 2010. *The Secret History of the World*. New York: Harry N. Abrams.
Burke, James. 1985. *The Day the Universe Changed*. New York: Little, Brown and Company.
Christian, David. 2005. *Maps of Time: An Introduction to Big History*. Berkeley: University of California Press.
———. 2008. *This Fleeting World: A Short History of Humanity*. London: Berkshire Publishing Group.
———. 2016. *Big History: Examines Our Past, Explains Our Present, Imagines Our Future*. London: DK.
———. 2018. *Origin Story: A Big History of Everything*. New York: Little, Brown and Company.
Crosby, Alfred. 1997. *The Measure of Reality: Quantification and Western Society: 1250–1600*. Cambridge: Cambridge University Press.
———. 2003. *The Columbian Exchange: Biological and Cultural Consequences of 1492*. Anniversary edition reprint. Santa Barbara: Praeger Press.
———. 2004. *Ecological Imperialism: The Biological Expansion of Europe, 900–1900*. Cambridge: Cambridge University Press.
Diamond, Jared. 2012. *The World Until Yesterday: What Can we Learn from Traditional Societies?* New York: Viking Press.
Fanon, Frantz. 2005. *The Wretched of the Earth*. Reprint. New York: Grove Press.
———. 2008. *Black Skin, White Masks*. Reprint. New York: Grove Press.
Faulkner, Neil. 2017. *A People's History of the Russian Revolution*. London: Pluto Press.
———. (2013) 2018. *A Radical History of the World*. London: Pluto Press.
Frankopan, Peter. 2015. *The Silk Roads: A New History of the World*. New York: Bloomsbury.
French, Howard. 2014. *China's Second Continent: How a Million Migrants Are Building a New Empire in Africa*. New York: Knopf.
———. 2018. *Everything Under the Heavens: How the Past Helps Shape China's Push for Global Power*. Visalia: Vintage.
Fukuyama, Francis. (1992) 2002. *The End of History and the Last Man*. Reprint. New York: Free Press.
———. 2011. *The Origins of Political Order: From Prehuman Times to the French Revolution*. New York: Farrar, Straus, and Giroux.
———. 2015. *Political Order and Political Decay: From the Industrial Revolution to the Globalization of Democracy*. New York: Farrar, Strauss, and Giroux.
Harman, Chris. (1999) 2018. *A People's History of the World: From the Stone Age to the New Millennium*. London: Verso.
Hume, David. 1975. *An Enquiry Concerning Human Understanding*. Reprint. Oxford: Oxford University Press.
Loewen, James. 1995. *Lies My Teacher Told Me: Everything Your American History Textbook Got Wrong*. New York: Touchstone.
Marx, Karl, and Engels, Fredrick. 1848. "The Communist Manifesto." https://www.marxists.org/archive/marx/works/download/pdf/Manifesto.pdf.

McNeill, William H. 1963. *The Rise of the West: A History of the Human Community.* Chicago: University of Chicago Press.

———. 1998. *A World History.* Reprint. Oxford: Oxford University Press.

Paine, Lincoln. 2015. *The Sea and Civilization: A Maritime History of the World.* Visalia: Vintage.

Pinker, Steven. 2011. *The Better Angels of Our Nature: Why Violence has Declined.* New York: Penguin Books.

Polybius. 2017. "On History." In *On Writing History: From Herodotus to Herodian*, edited by John Marincola, 53. New York: Penguin Classics.

Pselius, Michael. 1979. *Fourteen Byzantine Rulers.* London: Penguin Classics.

Raphael, Ray. 2016. *A People's History of the American Revolution: How Common People Shaped the Fight for Independence.* Reprint. New York: The New Press.

Schweitzer, Albert. 1906. *The Quest of the Historical Jesus.* Seattle: Thriftbooks.

Shermer, Michael. 2015. *The Moral Arc: How Science Leads Humanity toward Truth, Justice, and Freedom.* New York: Henry Holt & Co.

Tuchman, Barbara. 2011. *A Distant Mirror: The Calamitous 14th Century.* Reprint. New York: Random House Reissue.

Watson, Peter. 2012. *The Great Divide: History and Human Nature in the Old World and the New.* London: Orion Publishing.

Weatherford, Jack. 2004. *Genghis Khan and the Making of the Modern World.* New York: Crown Publishers.

Wells, H. G. 1920. *The Outline of History.* London: George Newnes.

Wilson, Edward O. (1994) 1998. *Consilience: The Unity of Knowledge.* Visalia: Vintage.

Woit, Peter. 2006. *Not Even Wrong: The Failure of String Theory and the Search for Unity in Physical Law.* New York: Basic Books.

Wollstonecraft, Mary. 2015. *A Vindication of the Rights of Women.* Reprint. London: Penguin Classics.

Zinn, Howard. (1980) 2015. *A People's History of the United States.* Reprint. New York: Harper Perennial.

About the Author

Dr. Chris Edwards is a veteran teacher of world history and Advanced Placement world history at a public high school in the Midwest and is the author of several books, including the five-volume *Connecting the Dots in World History* series published by R&L Education. He is a frequent contributor to *Skeptic* magazine on the topics of law, logic, psychology, theoretical physics, and education. Chris directs a generous grant from the Scientech Foundation for a Summer Institute for Math and Science Teachers through Ball State University. His teaching methodology and scholarship have been published by the National Council for Social Studies (NCSS) and the National Council for History Education. He has presented his teaching methodology to a national audience through a two-part webinar series hosted by the NCSS.

www.ingramcontent.com/pod-product-compliance
Lightning Source LLC
Chambersburg PA
CBHW030141240426
43672CB00005B/215